VALENTINO ROSSI

LIFE OF A LEGEND
Revised and Updated

MICHAEL SCOTT
FOREWORD BY WAYNE RAINEY,
World Champion 1990, 1991, 1992

motorbooks

Inspiring | Educating | Creating | Entertaining

Brimming with creative inspiration, how-to projects, and useful information to enrich your everyday life, Quarto.com is a favorite destination for those pursuing their interests and passions.

Second edition published in 2022
First published in 2017 by Motorbooks, an imprint of The Quarto Group,
100 Cummings Center, Suite 265-D, Beverly, MA 01915, USA.
T (978) 282-9590 F (978) 283-2742 Quarto.com

Motorbooks titles are also available at discount for retail, wholesale, promotional, and bulk purchase. For details, contact the Special Sales Manager by email at specialsales@quarto.com or by mail at The Quarto Group, Attn: Special Sales Manager, 100 Cummings Center, Suite 265-D, Beverly, MA 01915, USA.

26 25 24 23 22   1 2 3 4 5

ISBN: 978-0-7603-7838-0

Digital edition published in 2022
eISBN: 978-0-7603-7839-7

Library of Congress Cataloging-in-Publication Data

Names: Scott, Michael, 1946- author.
Title: Valentino Rossi : life of a legend / Michael Scott.
Description: Minneapolis, Minnesota : Motorbooks, an imprint of The Quarto
   Group, 2017. | Includes index.
Identifiers: LCCN 2017033894 | ISBN 9780760357385 (hardcover)
Subjects: LCSH: Rossi, Valentino. | Motorcyclists--Biography. | Motorcycle
   racing--History.
Classification: LCC GV1060.2.R65 S43 2017 | DDC 796.7/5092 [B] --dc23
LC record available at https://lccn.loc.gov/2017033894

Acquiring Editor: Darwin Holmstrom
Project Manager: Alyssa Lochner
Art Direction and Cover Design: Cindy Samargia Laun
Page Design and Layout: Simon Larkin

Printed in China

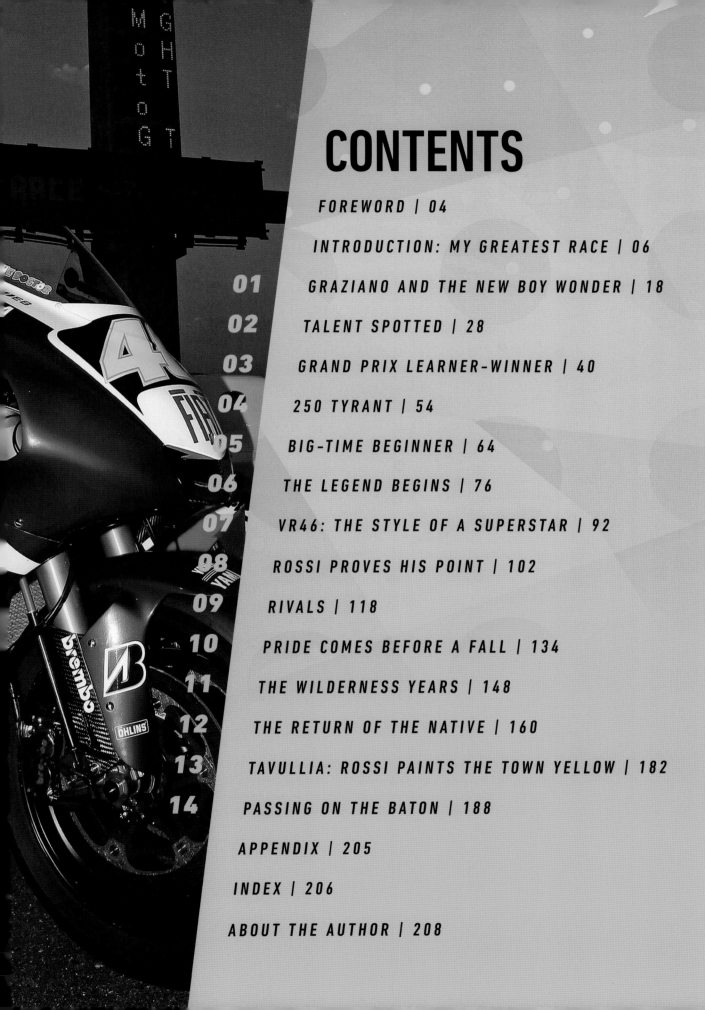

CONTENTS

FOREWORD

by Wayne Rainey

As a former Grand Prix racer, I know what it takes to wake up every day and put in the effort to improve yourself and be the best. The fans only see what happens on Sunday. They don't see the packed travel schedule, the training, and the countless days of testing and engineering and then re-engineering a bike to be a championship winner. There is so much work that goes on behind the scenes before the big race.

Valentino made it look easy. It always looked like he was having a good time. He just has that charisma. He was the guy you rooted for, and who was a lot of fun to watch. As a very clever and cunning racer he really handed it to his rivals on the track.

With such a long career, he successfully changed his program several times, incorporating new ideas to keep himself fresh and competitive against the constant flow of new competitors and technology developments, like electronic rider aids—and always to keep himself on, or near, the podium.

He went from Honda to Yamaha to Ducati and back to Yamaha again. I understand that. When I was racing for Yamaha and I had that chance to go to other teams, a few were really close decisions. So, I understand the motivation that drove Rossi to take on new challenges with different factories, different bikes, and different teammates.

He didn't make a lot of mistakes, even though he was on the bike all those years ... riding, racing, and testing and always at 95 percent-plus of his capabilities. He had so much talent he could ride on the very edge and avoid disaster. He was just so good.

As he started to get older a new generation of riders naturally emerged—Casey Stoner, Marc Marquez, and his teammate Jorge Lorenzo—and became real threats. He had to fight harder for his later race wins and championships. The constant effort he demonstrated to improve himself is what makes a champion.

I'm happy he was able to retire healthy and walk away. Staying there and being relevant for as long as he did ... I don't know if there'll be another rider like him for a long time.

Wayne Rainey

WAYNE RAINEY *was 500cc World Champion from 1990 to 1992 and set for a classic fourth in a row when a cruel crash ended his career. Yamaha's next title winner was Valentino Rossi, in 2004. A Hall of Fame inductee in the US and Europe and now president of US road-racing promoters MotoAmerica, charged with returning US riders to world prominence, Rainey remains a highly respected figure in world motorcycle racing.*

↑

*Triple-champion Wayne Rainey
leads Marlboro Yamaha teammate
Luca Cadalora in 1993.*

←

*In 1989, his second 500cc season,
Wayne was already a title
challenger.*

← ←

*Wayne Rainey as team owner,
after his retirement. Today he runs
MotoAmerica, the US road-racing
series. challenger.*

MY GREATEST RACE

Motorcycle racers are ordinary people—with extraordinary talent. This talent has many facets beyond the motor skills, coordination, and understanding of the dynamic possibilities of an overpowered assembly of metal, carbon fiber, and rubber.

→

One of Valentino Rossi's most amazing races was when he beat Casey Stoner at the US Grand Prix in 2008, a race that included one of the wildest passes ever attempted at Laguna Seca's infamous Corkscrew.

↑

Over more than two decades, Rossi went from teenage tearaway to respected paddock elder.

→

Andrea Dovizioso took over from Rossi at Ducati.

Courage is an obvious example of what makes a racer talented. A less obvious quality is persistence: the capacity to dig deep into one's reserves weekend after weekend, year after year. This is the facet that generally wears out first. Racers seldom retire because they've forgotten how to go fast; instead, it's the will to keep going that time saps away.

Then we have Valentino Rossi.

Several years past the age where most of his rivals had retired to enjoy the fruits of their high-risk, high-intensity occupation, Valentino Rossi continued to prove some-thing. Not that he is a great racer. Not that he is a major sporting personality, one of the biggest earners in any sport. Not that he is different from those rivals. Or, at least, not only these things.

He continued to prove that he still loved racing and still believed he could be competitive. In 2021, at the age of 41, facing a whole new generation of purpose-made talent—riders who had grown up with Rossi's picture pinned on their bedroom walls—he was still a podium finisher. Finally, in 2021, he ran a swan-song season, as without question the most popular rider on the grid.

In 26 years of World Championship Grand Prix racing, Rossi was the man.

The son of a Grand Prix winner, Graziano Rossi, Valentino was more or less raised to race. The younger Rossi's career wasn't driven by some paternal plan for world domination, as was the case with his great rival, Jorge Lorenzo. For Graziano, his own career cut short by injury, playing with bikes, go karts, and cars was just how he enjoyed himself. Valentino grew up sharing the pleasure. A bicycle gave way to a minibike, a go kart to a two-wheeled "pocket racer." These pastimes combined Rossi's natural talent with a charmed support that secured the best equipment for him. Long before coming of age, he had far outstripped his father.

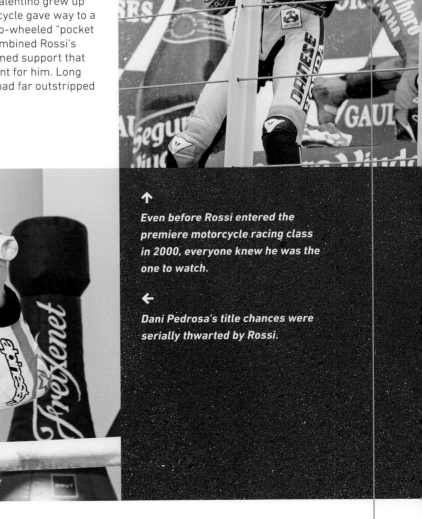

↑
Even before Rossi entered the premiere motorcycle racing class in 2000, everyone knew he was the one to watch.

←
Dani Pedrosa's title chances were serially thwarted by Rossi.

A kid from the hills just inland from the Rimini Riviera, Italy's holiday coast on the Adriatic, Valentino would break many racing records and establish new ones as he rapidly made his way to the premier Grand Prix class, first on temperamental 500cc two-strokes and then on brutishly fast 1000cc four-stroke machines. One record was for persistence. One race before the 2017 Austin round, in Argentina, he had made a record 350th start. His nearest rivals who are still active, Spain's Dani Pedrosa and fellow Italian Andrea Dovizioso (both former champions), were respectively 89 and 90 races behind him. Rossi had long since displaced previous record holder Alex Barros from Brazil, with 276 Grand Prix starts.

Rossi's response at the time was characteristically casual. "The number of races is not very important. It is the quality—the number of victories and podiums."

One record remained: the overall number of race victories. While Valentino makes light of it, this had been tantalizingly close for a couple of years. Compatriot Giacomo Agostini ("Ago"), multiple World Champion of the 1960s and 1970s, racked up 122 races wins, sometimes taking two a day on his dominant MV Agustas. Rossi's total, after adding another in 2017, stood at 115.

Quality remains a key word. While Ago took the majority of his wins on a machine head and shoulders above the rest, this has never been the case for Rossi. Sometimes his talent (and, to be honest, some special tires) meant he was able to play with his rivals, well aware of the value of making a good show of it. But many of his greatest victories have come against the odds.

One famous victory was in 2008 against reigning World Champion Casey Stoner's Ducati, at twisty Laguna Seca in California. Stoner had started from pole position and proved equal to all of Rossi's challenges. In response, Rossi showed his creative side—and his willingness to go close to the limits of legality—with a bold, borderline dive across the dirt on the inside of the second part of the famous Corkscrew corner.

Another landmark move had taken place at the scenic seaside Phillip Island circuit for the Australian Grand Prix five years earlier. Unsighted, Rossi made an illegal overtake under yellow "caution" flags after an accident. Officials slapped him with a ten-second time penalty; Rossi got the message on his pit signal board. With no time to battle Loris Capirossi's Ducati to make a good show, the Yamaha rider produced a spectacle: riding on the limit, he nullified the ten-second penalty, then added a five-second cushion.

→

Graziano says he didn't push Valentino into racing, but he certainly didn't discourage it.

↑

Rossi broke some, but not all, of the racing records set by Giacomo Agostini.

←

Rossi's father, Graziano, watched his son live out the glory he could never achieve.

↑
Ago first made a name for himself racing for MV Agusta.

→
Ago made history when he switched from MV Agusta to Yamaha and won a championship for the tuning-fork company.

←
Ago remains an honored senior citizen of the Grand Prix circus.

In Rossi's own mind, however, one race stands out. In one afternoon of skill and brinkmanship, he took his new Yamaha from underdog to top dog, proving what he'd been telling his former employers at Honda for the past four years: that the rider made the difference, not the motorcycle.

By the time Rossi got to the top class in 2000, he had already established a pattern: one year to learn (with race victories part of the process), one year to win. He spent two years in the entry-level 125 class, and two in the intermediate 250 class, taking a title in each for Aprilia.

Honda, the biggest fish in the big-bike pond, had snapped him up. He inherited the hugely successful pit crew of five-time champion Mick Doohan, who had been eliminated by injury, and did the same on the fearsome four-cylinder, two-stroke Honda NSR500: a year to learn, a year to win.

And he'd gone on winning. When the premier class underwent a cataclysmic technical change to the MotoGP four-strokes (at that time 990cc), he earned two more titles on Honda's V-5 masterpiece. But he missed the feisty lightweight 500 two-strokes, and there was something else that was wrong. It was personal: he didn't feel appreciated.

Rossi wasn't the first rider to find Honda an austere employer. It was partly due to the company's rigid management structure, but more an ingrained attitude of superiority. Honda had achieved greatness in the first place thanks to the quality of its engineering, developed in racing, and this remained the company ethic. The assumption was that Honda's engineers won races and championships.

As Rossi's longtime crew chief Jerry Burgess often said: "To Honda, riders are like lightbulbs. When one gets worn out, you just screw another one in."

This didn't sit well with Rossi, full of Italian emotion and pride. "Call it ego if you want," he wrote in his 2005 autobiography, *What If I Had Never Tried It*. Honda raced "to show [that] their bike and their company was better. I felt somewhat trapped by this attitude . . . perhaps that's why relations with the Honda executives had become somewhat tense."

There was a point to be proved, "that the rider was more important than the bike."

In 2003, Rossi had flirted with Ducati and been secretly wooed by Yamaha. After a series of clandestine meetings and secret negotiations, the latter won his signature.

There was just one problem: up against Honda's mighty V-5 as well as the very fast V-4 Ducati, Yamaha's M1 racer was clearly the underdog.

Rossi is a master at psychological warfare. In 2008 he used every trick in his bag to regain the championship from Stoner. These tactics had mentally destroyed many of Rossi's previous rivals, but Stoner is as strong as Rossi is cunning and would recover nicely.

Celebrating that first Yamaha win in South Africa, Valentino could hardly contain himself. He'd proved his point.

In 2002 Rossi had thrashed deadly rival Max Biaggi's top Yamaha by almost 150 points. In 2003, the best Yamaha, ridden by Carlos Checa, had been a distant seventh.

In late 2004, Rossi told me: "I was worried about everything, but I moved especially for my personal motivation. With Honda, I'd already won three championships in a row. To stay another two years would have been a fight for me, to work for something that I had already done."

Masao Furusawa, Yamaha's race department chief, had promised him technical improvements. When Rossi signed, though, he hadn't realized that the revered engineer was working on a brainwave.

Yamaha's bike, like their sports streetbikes, had a conventional inline four-cylinder engine, which endowed it with evenly spaced firing strokes. It is a compact engine, with advantages in simpler valve gear and lighter weight. Its rivals' Vee configurations were limited in these areas, but they meant an off-beat pattern of power strokes. For complex technical reasons—including crankshaft harmonics and tire performance—this meant Yamaha's competitors had better grip, which in turn meant better acceleration.

Furusawa's stroke of genius was to borrow crankshaft technology from American V-8 car engines, rearranging the big ends at 90-degree intervals with a so-called "cross-plane" crankshaft. Without changing the bike's outward appearance—and without sacrificing its other advantages—he had turned the M1 Yamaha from a smooth-firing in-line engine into a virtual V-4.

Honda banned Rossi from testing the Yamaha until the end of the calendar year, when his contract expired. This left less than four months before the opening round, which would take place on the South African Highveld outside the gold-mining town of Welkom—only four months to get a brand-new engine ready to race.

There was plenty of work to be done—for the rider, the factory engineers, and Rossi's Burgess-led pit crew, who had come with him from Honda. They set to it with a will.

One significant change was to raise the center of gravity, which made the bike pitch more under acceleration and braking. This worked better with Rossi's style of moving a lot on his bike and using the bike's movement underneath him.

All too soon, it was race time. Nobody on the team expected to win at the high-altitude Phakisa Freeway. After all, while Rossi had taken the victory there on his second visit in 2001 on the Honda two-stroke, he'd been beaten (if narrowly) on his two subsequent visits to the course in the next two years.

As the 2004 event started, Rossi took pole in the final scramble on qualifying tires, just 0.035 of a second ahead of the Hondas of Sete Gibernau and Max Biaggi.

"It's like ten pole positions on a Honda—like a victory," Rossi said, showing the strain of the effort. The challenge was plain to see: the Yamaha lacked ultimate top speed on the long straight. It was nimble, though, and it responded to his input on crucial suspension and geometry settings.

←

The race of his life. Rossi, first time on a Yamaha, won the opening round of 2004 from Biaggi's Honda by two tenths of a second.

The 2.6-mile lap closed on a series of tight bends. If he could get to them first on the last of the twenty-eight laps, perhaps he could take the advantage.

Rossi's Yamaha led away, with the previous year's winner Gibernau second. Before half a lap, though, ex-Yamaha team leader Biaggi was leaning on Rossi. They'd swapped bikes; now they were swapping paint.

On lap four, the yellow Honda was ahead. Rossi's Gauloises-blue Yamaha passed straight back.

There followed a relentless fast-paced game of cat-and-mouse. Over and over, Biaggi would close right up on Rossi, especially on the back straight. He looked comfortable, and, with half the course complete, it seemed that Rossi—hopping under braking and sliding under power—might have to surrender.

But that's never an option for Rossi, and his natural race-craft told him he was faster through the closing tight corners. Never give up.

With six laps to go, Biaggi attacked. He surged past on the straight and held the advantage through the twists, embarking on an attempted breakaway. Now, however, you could see he was right on the limit.

Rossi's counterattack came with two laps left: he dove inside the Honda at the penultimate corner in a classic block pass. Still, he had no more success in breaking away than his rival.

It was hard for spectators to draw breath in the final lap, to say nothing of what the riders were going through. Rossi was three-tenths ahead at the start of it, and Biaggi set a new lap record as he chased. But Rossi was always out of reach.

He crossed the line to win by just over two-tenths of a second. He had won at his first attempt on the underdog Yamaha, making history: the first rider to win back-to-back races on different makes of motorcycle.

Ever the showman, Rossi had established a pattern of celebrating his race wins with elaborate costume pantomimes, contrived in league with his fan club. There would be no such tableaux at Welkom.

Instead, halfway round, he pulled over, leaned the bike against the tire barrier, and sat down in front of it, cradling his head, his shoulders tumbling. It looked as though he was crying with relief. A year later, he revealed the truth: "I was laughing."

Rossi went on to win the title, his fourth in a row. Only Geoff Duke, Giacomo Agostini, and Eddie Lawson had won championships on different makes, and only Lawson did so in consecutive years. More: it was Yamaha's first championship since 1992. Rossi had proved it. It was the rider who won, not the motorcycle.

CHAPTER 01

GRAZIANO AND THE NEW BOY WONDER

The Teenage Mutant Ninja Turtle clings to the back of a dome, peering over the top. His orange mask proclaims him to be Michelangelo (he provides comic relief, according to one synopsis, "but still has an adventurous side"). But he's moving too fast for one to be really sure. On every side, there's a flail of knees and elbows, and the weedy drone of tiny motorcycle engines.

→

Valentino Rossi was born into a racing family on February 16, 1979.

The dome is a Kevin Schwantz replica helmet. Inside is one of the spectacular Texan racer's biggest fans—a twelve-year-old Valentino Rossi. He's about to take the first of many victories in the brawling series of pocket-bike "Minimoto" races that served the bike-mad youth of the Adriatic holiday coast.

The turtle remained an iconic image: Rossi eventually had one tattooed on his belly. And it was here, on the countless go-kart tracks in towns along the coast—and even in town squares or supermarket car parks cordoned off with tape and bales—that some of the greatest motorcycle racing talent of the subsequent twenty years cut its teeth and earned spurs.

Rossi was at the forefront. He was already showing a precocious talent, along with gift for racing that was more than just a drive to win or to capture glory. According to his father, he was doing it for the sheer pleasure of the race.

He'd inherited this from Graziano. But there was something extra in the junior Rossi: he also had a real killer instinct. That, said Graziano, was what led him to a string of World Championships, often in the company of his own pre-teen companions from the Minimoto circus.

The Adriatic holiday coast where Valentino grew up is steeped in two-wheeled history, tradition, and action. It's only a slight exaggeration when Graziano describes the provincial capital Pesaro, less than 20 miles farther down the coast, as "the capital of motorcycling." Here the famous racing Benellis were made, and the innovative Motobi road bikes. It was for another enthusiast-manufacturer,

Rossi's father, Graziano, had once been an aspiring motorcycle racer but had his career cut short by injuries.

Agostini earned the status of legend by winning championships for MV Agusta. The Italian set a benchmark; Rossi never quite caught up.

Ago in his pomp.
He and Valentino are
both legends in their
native Italy.

Morbidelli, for whom Graziano himself raced, winning the first of three Grands Prix in 1979 (finishing third overall in the 250cc class) with the number 46—something else his son would inherit. Known for his adventurous (read "scary") style, Graziano moved on to factory Suzukis, then Yamaha 500cc bikes. He would have continued but for a series of head injuries (one sustained in a rally-car crash) that cut his two-wheel career short in 1982. He kept competing on four wheels, but never at the same level as he had experienced in his motorcycle racing career.

Graziano had married his childhood neighbor Stefania, a primary school teacher, in 1978. Valentino was born on February 16, 1979, in the walled city of Urbino, inland from the town of Tavullia, where the family lived. He was christened not in honor of Saint Valentine's Day, but in memory of

his father's close friend; this Valentino had helped Graziano build his first competition motorcycle, but he later died in a drowning accident. His son would have been Valentino, Graziano explained, "even if he had been born in December."

Graziano and Stefania divorced in 1990, and eleven-year-old Valentino moved with his mother to Montecchio, less than five miles south of Tavullia.

There was no separation between father and son, however, and their adventures with horsepower and wheels continued apace. Graziano was still friends with several Grand Prix racers, and Rossi Junior was familiar with the championship paddock from his earliest years. Later, when he defeated veteran multiple champion Jorge "Aspar" Martinez in the 125 class, the Spaniard joked: "I should have run over him when I had the chance."

↑

Graziano raced in a day when even world champions like Agostini slept in the back of vans on race weekends. Graziano would follow that ethic even after his son was earning millions.

→

Racing in the 1980s. Randy Mamola leads a pack of two-strokes. Graziano's somewhere among the pursuers.

Ago, here on a Yamaha, was one of four riders to win the premier crown on different makes. But only Rossi and Californian Eddie Lawson did it in consecutive years.

Most racing fans believed that Ago's records would never fall. Rossi would see that as a challenge.

↑

*Intimations of immortality?
Young Valentino tries his father's
Bimota Grand Prix bike for size.*

→

*Young Rossi showed affinity
for anything with wheels.*

Like many European kids born into racing families, Rossi got his start in kart racing at a very early age. But bikes were more fun.

Valentino lived the life of a typical teenage rascal, and later wrote in his autobiography about madcap escapades with his group of friends, "the tribe." Their antics mainly involved tearing around at high speeds, often pursued by the local police, who frequently confiscated their vehicles. In Italy, it was legal to ride 50cc scooters or mopeds from the age of fourteen, provided they limited their speed to under 45 kilometers per hour. The speed governors were the first casualty of the tribe's handy wrenches, and the boys took advantage of a wide range of hop-up parts to get their rides to do at least double that speed.

As Rossi later recalled, from the age of fourteen to eighteen they would race "all day and every day": by night on their own informally drawn track in an industrial park, and by day along the 22-kilometer SP44—the "Strada Panoramica"—a coast road through the seaside mountains between Gabicce Monte and Pesaro. All this, in addition to Valentino's formal racing career, which by then had already been going for four years.

Valentino first rode a motorcycle at the age of two, with safety wheels that were removed within three days. His parents kept his early racing on four wheels, with a go kart, and, by the time he was old enough to race formally at the age of ten, he was already accomplished at the arts of power-sliding and forceful overtaking, having been practicing these moves since he was five. These skills he learned playing with Graziano and his friends, including later Grand Prix winners Loris Reggiani and Luca Cadalora. The latter, a double-250 champion, joined Rossi in 2016 as his "rider coach."

→

Rossi jumped at the chance to compete in the increasingly popular sport of Minimoto racing.

↓

Rossi's infectious smile soon became a fixture at Italian racetracks.

The playground was a local quarry or gravel pit—one they settled at after being banned from a number of others—where they made circuits for Valentino's kart and their own dirt bikes, and kicked up dust to their hearts' content. The lessons of how to drive, and also to ride sideways, would bear much more fruit than Valentino's formal schooling, which he abandoned as soon as he could step into the role of teenage professional racer. In future years, Graziano and Valentino established a more elaborate training ranch near Tavullia, with oval and switchback dirt tracks, to train a new generation of Italian riders at the VR46 Ranch.

Valentino wanted to race his kart before he was eligible, but a roguish attempt to forge the necessary documentation when he was still only nine went wrong, and he had to wait. Success in the junior classes came quickly: his first race was in 1989, and, in 1990, he won the junior regional championship. Typical Rossi: one year to learn, one year to win.

By now, though, there was another interest. Minimoto racing had begun in 1989, and Valentino fell deeply under its spell. It was here, he explained, that he learned about close racing, how to be aggressive, how to overtake. "There would usually be four or five guys racing." He also learned how much he enjoyed it. When the time came to decide whether to pursue his karting career, which would have strained the family budget, or to concentrate on two wheels, the money didn't come into it, according to Valentino. Bikes, he has always made very clear, "were not my second choice."

In 1991, he won his first Minimoto race. His future was clear in his own mind.

↑

Graziano's influence opened doors for his son's career. The kid made the most of them.

←

Aprilia Cup, and new kid Valentino leads. He was competitive from the start.

CHAPTER 02

TALENT SPOTTED

It's not what you know, but who you know. The cliché isn't quite strong enough to cover the case of Valentino. He got his first breaks in racing because of the who-you-know factor—or, at least, who his father Graziano knew. But he made the most of what he knew, and what he could do.

→

"My eyes when braking at the end of the straightaway." Rossi mugs for a mug shot.

By 1992, he certainly knew what he wanted to do: keep on racing motorcycles.

With the Minimotos, he was already half-way there. Still too young for a racing licence for full-size bikes on full-size tracks—the minimum age was fourteen—he had made his own contacts, persuading a friend to lend him his Aprilia 125 (and, for official purposes, his identity) for an underage track-day outing at the Misano Adriatico circuit. This was his local track—and also a world-class Grand Prix venue. He found the experience sobering, but, more importantly, utterly entrancing.

Wearing borrowed leathers and his Schwantz replica helmet on a cold November day, his first laps on the "Sport Production" Aprilia (a street bike stripped down and tuned up for a junior race series) were tentative. It was the biggest, heaviest bike the thirteen-year-old had ridden, and it was the first time he'd had to cope with a clutch and gears.

If he didn't set the track on fire, though, he lit a blaze within himself: discovering how the focus and perspective change on a closed circuit, how the sinuous tarmac swims in front of your eyes, becomes the only reality, while everything else merges into the distance. It opened up a world of fascinating possibilities.

He told his father and his somewhat dismayed mother: "I want to race motorcycles."

Graziano set the wheels in motion, calling his old friend and rival Virginio Ferrari with a request: "We need to find a bike for Valentino."

→

Home on the road: teenage Vale's motorhome was generally messy, almost always happy.

Halfway there: Valentino's flowing locks were an early trademark.

Be careful. There's a party animal about!

Drink it down-down-down: Rossi and
best friend Uccio knew how to party.

↖
Friendship: almost as important as winning. A young Valentino and "Uccio" Salucci.

↓

Racing's just a game, and games are just racing. Both are taken seriously.

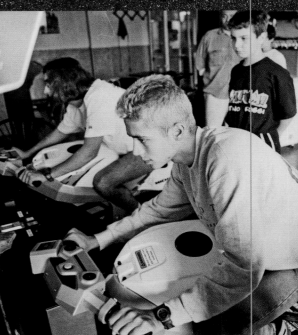

Ferrari had been 500cc championship runner up to "King Kenny" Roberts in 1979. Now retired, he was managing the Ducati World Superbike team. Ducati had recently become the property of Cagiva, itself owned by the Castiglione family. Virginio called Claudio Castiglione, who in turn gave the order to Claudio Lusuardi, who ran the official factory team in the Sport Production series.

Voilà. The novice from the seaside Minimoto circus was starting his career in a works team.

This sounds grander than it actually was: the Cagiva Mito was still just a tuned production bike, and Valentino was very much the team junior, last on the list for special upgrades. This inclusion of the young Rossi on the team remains important, though, both symbolically and prac-

tically. First, it proved what sort of doors Valentino's background could open for him. Second, at the very least he would have access to a competent motorcycle—one that somebody else had paid for.

All the fourteen-year-old had to do was prove he was worthy of the privilege.

History records an unpromising start. "I fell off on the first corner," explains Valentino, with a trademark cheeky grin.

It happened at Magione, a small circuit some two hours into the mountains southwest of Rossi's home. Valentino was practicing for his first race on the Cagiva. Out he went, cold spring morning, cold tires, and pitched it into the corner. And he was down. It took a while to fix the damage, and out he went again. This time, he recalled, "I made three or four laps." Then he crashed again.

Many might have seen the writing on the wall. Not Valentino. He was depressed, of course. But he wasn't about to give up. Without realizing it at the time, he was establishing his own modus operandi: push hard early on to find the limit; then, having done so, remember it well. If you have exceptional ability, then you can keep going right up to the point you lose control, then stop short just before disaster. That's how you learn to go as fast as a motorcycle will let you.

Rossi finished ninth in the race and competed for a full season, ultimately finishing third overall behind two future Grand Prix stars: Andrea Ballerini and 2000 125cc champion Roberto Locatelli. By the end of it, in the final at his home track of

Misano, he was offered teammate Ballerini's spare "works" bike. He put on pole position and finished on the podium.

One year to learn.

Thus, as he established the pattern, 1994 would be the year to win.

That year, now with the official Cagiva Mito in the same factory-backed team, Valentino won his first race at the historic Italian cathedral of speed at Monza, going on to take the Sport Production title. This wasn't a given, though, and his title was only awarded him after a series of protests and official intervention recompensed him for having been knocked wide on the last corner of the series finale. His assailant was eventually disqualified, and Rossi had enough points for his first national championship.

↑
Trying to look innocent, but this youngster was made for mischief.

←
Rossi never had to work on his image. His personality did it for him.

→
Back where it started. Rossi would outgrow play bikes and scooters, but would never stop playing.

→ *Valentino's first races were on a go kart. That's him on the screen. But he chose two wheels.*

Also in 1994, he campaigned a full racing bike in the Italian 125cc championship on a specially built chassis called a Sandroni, created by a Pesaro enthusiast and friend of Graziano's. It was powered by an Aprilia-Rotax engine, thanks to Aprilia racing boss Carlo Pernat, another old friend—and someone who would later become a major benefactor. Pernat, still involved as a rider manager and fixer in 2017, hardly needed the benefit of hindsight to say, "I could see from the beginning that Valentino had a very special talent."

Still learning, but learning fast. The Sandroni gave him the chance to ride on full-race slick tires while also putting him up against higher-level opposition, including World Championship riders "slumming" in the national series. They showed him the possibilities, and gave him a target as he devoted his energies to learning.

Speaking of learning, Rossi's school career suffered in direct proportion to his racing successes. He was missing more and more lessons to travel to races, and getting used to the usual comments from teachers about how "you'll never make a living riding round and round on your motorbikes."

Oh, really?

The absences got longer in 1995, culminating in the end of his studies at the age of fifteen. That year, he fulfilled his usual promise, winning the national 125 title at his second attempt. More importantly, he was now travelling outside Italy to race, on a production-racer RS125R Aprilia laid on by Pernat, in the European Championship.

That series is now extinct, but at the time it was an important steppingstone to the World Championships. The races, most importantly, were actually run as support events—usually on Saturday—at Grand Prix

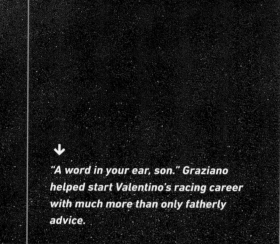

"A word in your ear, son." Graziano helped start Valentino's racing career with much more than only fatherly advice.

weekends. Rossi was soon getting noticed as the pushy youngster who crashed a lot. But he was also fast enough when he did finish to claim third overall.

The European series gave him a great deal, he later explained. They gave him a chance to learn the circuits he would soon be facing as a World Championship contender, and to regain a place in the paddock society he had known as a young child.

It was also a chance to assess the task, to see firsthand the speed of those who'd already graduated to Grand Prix level. "I realized that the riders were very fast, and I had a lot to learn," he told me a few years later. At some tracks, they were four or

more seconds per lap faster than his own time on the over-the-counter Aprilia, but he took the time to go trackside and study the corner lines and techniques they used to get there.

In a way, this was an end to pure fun racing for Rossi. In the Italian domestic series, rivalry on the track had been fierce, but the riders played just as hard together when the racing was over. World Championship racing was a more serious, more time-consuming pursuit. The social side was muted, the racing deadly earnest, in line with the size of the prizes.

Rossi was up for the challenge.

Valentino's half-brother Luca Marini would follow him into Grand Prix racing in the new century. It helps to start learning young.

Breakfast of champions. Or just one champion, many times over.

Born with a silver spoon in his mouth? Luca would have the best possible mentor for his future racing career.

GRAND PRIX LEARNER– WINNER

Minimoto racing meant much more than its size suggested. In Japan, they were called "pocket-bikes," feeding a juvenile racing scene that was even more active than on the Adriatic coast. Consequently, they fulfilled something of a national dream for the country that made most of the machines used in racing, from miniature to full-sized, as a generation of frighteningly competitive schoolboy racers grew up and moved onto the world stage.

→

After an early win, Rossi fans make sure his feet don't touch the ground.

→

Eyes on the prize. Rossi came into GP racing with no illusions. He knew he could learn to win.

↓

The fan club had its own ritual: finding new ways to celebrate Rossi's new world.

Honda fielded Japan's first tentative entry into Grand Prix racing in 1959. Within two years came the first championship, immediately followed by Yamaha, Suzuki, and Kawasaki. The silverware kept piling up in the factory cabinets. All that was missing were Japanese *riders* to complete the set. There'd been just one exception, Takazumi Katayama, who took a single 350cc title in 1977.

Minimoto changed that. As the 1990s wore on, the 125cc class became increasingly like a Japanese national championship, with a new generation of small-class samurai elbowing aside the usual Italian and Spanish riders. Nobbie Ueda took two wins in 1991; by 1993, four of the top six were Japanese; a year later came a top-three lockout. Tough little Kazuto Sakata was champion, Ueda second, and Masaki Tokudome third. In 1995, Haru Aoki won the first of two consecutive titles, Sakata second, and Saito fourth; next year, another top three, with Tokudome and Manako placing second and third.

By now, they'd been joined by an ebullient Italian teenager who loved their close-combat riding style and enjoyed their company off-track, too. Valentino took their measure and interrupted Japan's reign in 1997—another example of his learning-year, winning-year style.

←

The ritual started early. At first, just to stretch the leathers; later because of what might happen if the ritual was abandoned.

During 1996, he wrote in his autobiography, he'd learned "that I did, in fact, have the ability to eventually win the championship."

His first season was with a new team that had been put together by the elegant and gentlemanly Gilera fan Giampiero Sacchi, a noted Italian racing Svengali and later team owner. At that time, Sacchi was involved with Aprilia, where Pernat was in charge, and had passed on the previous year's factory bike.

Rossi had a lot of fun. "That was me at my craziest. I really was an absolute pest. I had no respect for anyone on the track." This attitude soon got him known to his fans and rivals alike, though not everyone found it quite as amusing. There were fifteen races that year, and the kid with the flowing locks and sun-and-moon helmet had at least fifteen crashes, most of them in practice. It was enough to dismay team boss Sacchi.

In a famous and oft-reported exchange after one of those crashes, Sacchi gave his rider a good talking to. He explained that, if Rossi kept carrying on like this, he could only hope to be another Kevin Schwantz (famed for win-or-crash derring-do), rather than taking after the smooth and efficient Max Biaggi, who that

The thirst for victory can't be slaked by champagne, no matter how hard you try.

In his early years, Rossi thought that journalists were his friends. That was before the story got out of control.

↑
The ecstasy and the ecstasy. No place for agony when teenage race-winner Vale meets his fans.

→
"I should have run him over when I had the chance." Veteran Jorge Martinez (left) has just been beaten by Rossi (center) at Mugello in 1997. Garry McCoy (right) was third. Martinez first met Rossi as a babe in arms.

year claimed the third of four consecutive 250cc crowns. It was the wrong example: Valentino already nurtured an antipathy for his compatriot, which later grew into the fiercest rivalry. "I thought—okay, then I will carry on like this."

In Austria that year, sixteen-year-old Ivan Goi, another Italian, became the youngest-ever Grand Prix winner. I wrote at the time:

Many were a little saddened that he'd denied the honor to Valentino Rossi, whose flamboyant personality, exotic appearance, and electrifying riding style combined to make him popular rookie of the year in any class, his antics the highlight of almost every weekend.

Valentino put himself with the front group from the first race, claiming his first podium in Austria, his first lap record in France, and his first historic victory at Brno in the Czech Republic. He finished ninth in the championship, having encountered many circuits for the first time. His racing career was on a roll.

So, too, was his career as an icon. Being noticeable just came naturally. He was funny and friendly, and it was impossible not to be aware of him. His silky long hair, centrally parted, shone like Prince Valiant's, while his

↗
That's Osvaldo the Chicken on the pillion, after winning in Catalunya in 1998— elaborating on an invented mystery sponsor prank Rossi had played on Italian TV.

←
"Hear ye, hear ye. I am come to be worshiped." Rossi works the crowd at an early fan event.

↘
Royalty meets royalty. Spain's King Juan Carlos, a bike racing fan, joins winner Rossi on the Jerez podium in 1997.

1997

→

Robin Hood hat at Donington Park, down the road from Sherwood Forest. This was win number nine, with Masaki Tokudome (left) second and Ueda (right) third. Japanese rivals gave rise to the Rossifumi nickname.

↓

Rossi's shows made his mark as an entertainer as a 125 rider. When he won the 250 title in 1999 in Brazil, his guardian angel joined his victory lap.

cackling laugh preceded him as he belted round the paddock on his scooter, making friends everywhere.

He was a natural showman, too. His battles with the Japanese and his enjoyment of their company led him to adopt a new nickname after his first Grand Prix win. It was on his leathers, on T-shirts, on his pit board: "Rossifumi," inspired by premier-class hero Norifumi Abe.

His personality shone out, and he seemed ubiquitous. That was just his nature. Later, he would understand how to harness it to make millions.

His second year in the beginner's class was a rout. He already knew he had the ability. Aprilia had beefed up his Sacchi-led team's personnel and given him the very latest factory bike.

There were fifteen rounds. Rossi won the first in Malaysia, followed by ten more. The only other rider to win was Japan's Nobbie Ueda, who finished a distant second in the championship. Some wins were close, some easier. Some were in the dry, others in the wet. Four were by less than a second: the closest by 0.1 of a second, at Assen. The largest was a very atypical six seconds over

↑
Promo duties: Rossi takes to the track on a production Aprilia RSV Mille at the big V-twin's launch. He was contracted to the factory until 1999.

←
Soaked at home at Imola. Rossi has just won again, from Manako and Kazuto Sakata (right).

Teenage GP rider Valentino looks hardly big enough for a grown-up crash helmet.

Vord Cienpion—it's a mock Japanese rendition, to go with the Rossifumi nickname. Rossi aside, Japanese riders dominated the 125 class.

Rossi tied up the 1997 125 World Championship at Brno, and his fan club was ready to celebrate.

Sakata in Catalonia. Notably, when Ueda beat him to second in Austria, it was by 0.004 of a second. He had only one non-finish, when he crashed (out of first place) at Suzuka, second race of the year.

The overall effect was emphatic. Valentino won the championship, as he knew he could, by a massive margin of more than eighty points, 321 to Ueda's 238.

It was during this year that Rossi-mania began. He didn't go into racing to become famous or rich. First and foremost, it was for fun. He didn't even enter his career to win, although it was winning that made it even more fun. And his open

nature and response to the crowd were part of the same game: a teenager having lots of fun.

Around this time, he started his famous post-race pantomimes—ready-prepared shows with his fan club, generally paying some tribute to the location or the situation. Like sporting Robin Hood's bow and arrow in Britain, close to Nottingham and Sherwood Forest. Or the Superman cape, emblazoned "Rossifumi," in the Netherlands.

Suddenly, though, his fame was out of control.

He'd always spent time laughing and joking with the Italian press at the circuit.

Rossi won his first World Championship at the same Brno track where he had won his first grand prix the previous year.

Winning was expected by round ten in Germany. His podium pals are Yoshi Katoh (left) and "Tex" Geissler.

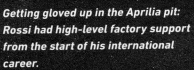
↑

Getting gloved up in the Aprilia pit: Rossi had high-level factory support from the start of his international career.

→

Proud father Graziano joins his son, the new World Champion.

Now he discovered that they weren't really his friends: he was a story, and that could go both ways. They could criticize as well as praise. In fact, they sold more papers if they criticized his performance.

It came home to him after he'd won the title in Brazil. He was at home in Tavullia celebrating in the break before the final flyaway rounds, enjoying a big party with seemingly all his old pals. They decided to go to a nightclub in Montecchio. Valentino was in the back of one of the cars, a Porsche 928, driven by his father Graziano, who typically decided to stop off at an industrial estate to test out how far sideways he could make it go. Something

went wrong, they rolled and hit a lamppost, and Valentino suffered a concussion. The next day, to his dismay, it was all over the national press, and they'd gotten the story all wrong. The papers declared that he'd been driving while under the influence. Shocked and embarrassed, Valentino learned from that incident to be careful of the press.

He could have moved up to the next class, 250cc, at the beginning of the year; but he wanted the 125 title first. Now there was no impediment. He needed to test himself on something a bit bigger and more powerful. But there was no guarantee it would work.

So great a cloud of witnesses, with so great a barrage of lenses.

Caps galore for the teenage World Champion.

CHAPTER 04

250 TYRANT

Rossi's transformation from 250 learner to graduate came after the twelfth of fourteen rounds of his first 250 season. He had just won the second of four races in a row, but this time he had started badly, finishing the first lap in thirteenth place. "I was riding smoothly and carefully after my bad start, only overtaking when it was really safe. I think it shows I am more mature now."

→

Aprilia 250 team new boy Rossi hounds teammate and eventual champion Loris Capirossi. Being top Aprilia was a major goal.

Much more mature, as a rider. As a showman, though, he was only just getting going. He celebrated that win by giving a friend in a chicken suit a pillion ride to *parc ferme*. But his post-race pantomimes were becoming eagerly anticipated by a fan base that was growing exponentially.

So too his hairstyle. He'd lost the flowing locks before the end of 1997 and was now turning up to races with his close-cropped hair dyed a variety of ever more elaborate colors: green in Britain, dazzling orange in the Netherlands (where his coincidental tribute to the national color was sweeter after his first victory), and a green-white-and-red *tricolore* (echoed in his helmet, leathers, and fairing) before winning his second home race at Imola.

All told, Rossi won five of fourteen races in 1998, including the last four in a row. He also crashed out of four of them, mainly earlier in the year. This showed how far he had brought his headlong approach to this new learning curve, as well as illustrating his ability to climb it rapidly.

Rossi had just turned nineteen when he lined up for his first 250 Grand Prix. As 125 champion, it was no surprise that he was taken straight into Aprilia's factory squad, alongside Japan's Tetsuya Harada and fellow Italian Loris Capirossi. It was a great year for the Italian factory, having taken the riders' title thrice in the past four years, and the team easily outranked the Japanese opposition in performance.

The factory team livery was black. The bikes predominately matched the color scheme, though Rossi's had bigger stripes of red displaying sponsor International Petroleum's logo and a broader white stripe emblazoned with the brand of beer producer Nastro Azzurro, a personal ally.

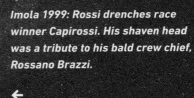

Imola 1999: Rossi drenches race winner Capirossi. His shaven head was a tribute to his bald crew chief, Rossano Brazzi.

Flip-flop through the Assen chicane: winner Capirossi is just out of Rossi's reach.

Rossi chases defending champion and ex-teammate Capirossi's Honda at Assen.

He was already becoming a big brand name in his own right—or at least the basis for this degree of recognition was well in place. Rossi-mania was already spreading around the world.

This posed difficulties. It was one thing to be the most famous person in Tavullia and environs. Old friends were running the increasingly popular fan club. Another old family associate, "Gibo" Badioli, was his manager. Even those on the periphery were friends, people with whom he felt comfortable. Tavullia could share in his success: already the town priest, Don Cesare, was in the habit of ringing the church bells every time Valentino won a race, a habit that continues to this day.

Away from his home turf, though, it was more difficult. Now he was recognized everywhere; complete strangers wanted to be his best friend. It was especially noticeable at the first Italian race of the year:

round four took place at Mugello, outside Florence in the Apennine foothills, where the paddock was beset by giggling gangs of teenage girls looking as though they were going to a Spice Girls concert—but they were intent on getting close to the new, far more interesting superstar.

I wrote at the time, "It is a tribute to the power of one person, with the right technical specifications, to galvanize, knowingly or not, a whole new level of spectator involvement." But we'd seen nothing yet. Nor had Rossi, although he had already been obliged to adopt a disguise to visit the Bologna motorcycle show to avoid being mobbed.

The racing, in retrospect, was the work of a young maestro: bold and skillful in equal measure. Rossi was not one to be overawed by the seniority of his teammates or his rivals, nor by his motorcycle's increased performance, with double the

The Australian GP was win number seven of nine in Valentino's championship year. The cockscomb hat? Don't ask.

→

All smiles on the podium in France, but there was tension inside the factory Aprilia team among class rookie Rossi, Tetsuya Harada (center), and Loris Capirossi.

←

Massive crowds
at Jerez in Spain
watch the dominant
Aprilia 250 trip:
Capirossi leading
Rossi and Harada.

↗
Close racing typified the front battle in 250s in 1998, with new boy Rossi always involved. Jeremy McWilliams and Rossi chase Capirossi in Germany.

horsepower of his relatively friendly 125: more weight, and much more speed.

Instead, while smiling on the outside, he later recorded a great deal of tension between the three different factions in the Aprilia squad, between the technicians, and, especially, the three riders. Their bikes outranked the opposition, but, for Rossi, "to come third was like coming last." Looking back, 1998 was a turning point and a difficult year, when he learned how to become not just serious about racing but actually ruthless.

Not that he needed many lessons in how to seize the psychological advantage. Consider his tactics at his first test on the 250: aware that all eyes would be on him, he quietly requested Dunlop to bring special supersoft, sticky tires. On these he set a blazing lap time. Point made: he was already faster than Biaggi, his Aprilia predecessor.

His technique also took a step. Racing a 125, he explained, was more like a bicycle. A 250 had enough power to make it slide. He had to learn how to use those slides to go faster. The bigger bike also burned its tires up over the course of a race; Rossi had to take that into account in his technique as much as in the delicate machine's setup. He also started physical training during the year after experiencing levels of effort and subsequent fatigue he'd never encountered on a 125. He was learning: racing was not *only* about setting a fast lap time.

He qualified seventh for the first round in Japan, one of only two times not in the front row, and broke down in the race. Next was Malaysia: the rookie led the early laps and crashed on the last while disputing the win with Harada. "When you have ridden a race like that, you have to try to win," he explained.

So on it went. At Jerez, Rossi led, but finished second; at Mugello, ditto; and at Paul Ricard, he came in second again.

↑

Tension on the grid at Imola in 1998: Harada, Rossi, and French future champion Olivier Jacque wait for release.

↓

Beach gear was meant to celebrate a win at Mugello. Rossi came second to Marcellino Lucchi (right), and was later embarrassed about stealing the older rider's rare chance in the limelight.

The Dutch TT was always a big race. Rossi, winner Capirossi, and third-place McWilliams enjoy the adulation of a huge crowd in 1999.

Then he had another crash (from the lead) at Jarama. His first win came at Assen, another crash in Britain, then he came in third in Germany before another crash, on lap one, in the Czech Republic. It was at this point that he gained true understanding.

There were four races left, and he won all of them, adding two more lap records to the one already recorded in Malaysia.

One year to learn—but a hell of a year. He was second overall, and twenty-three points behind Capirossi. If just one of those crashes while leading hadn't happened, he'd have been champion.

In the 500 class, multi-250 champion Max Biaggi had a similar experience, losing his first title to the dominant Mick Doohan. Max was the biggest motorcycling star in Italy—Rossi didn't like that. Asked once if considered himself "the Biaggi of 250s," he replied that he'd rather think that "Biaggi might be the Rossi of the 500s." This feud would only ripen in the coming years.

There would be no ifs or buts for Rossi in 1999. There were no crashes in sixteen races, and only one non-finish, when his chain came off in France. He showed some unexpected caution with seventh in round two at a sodden Motegi circuit in Japan, saying, "I prefer to ride my motorcycle on dry land." He was also eighth at rain-hit Valencia. Apart from these instances—and after a misfire had him fifth in round one in Malaysia—Rossi was never off the podium. Nine wins, two second places, and one third (after he had already secured the crown) was clear proof of his stature.

He had invented a new alter ego for the season, laying Rossifumi to rest and bringing to life Valentinik, based on Paperinik, a lovable Disney-style, cape-wearing superhero, based in turn on Paperino, the Italian name for Donald Duck. "I needed something new after the difficulties of 1998," he explained.

And to prepare him for his next challenge: full-size racing on the awe-inspiring 500cc two-strokes of the premier class.

World Champion elect: Rossi won again in Great Britain in 1999, ahead of Capirossi (left) and Nakano.

Top three in the TT: Winner Capirossi and runner up Rossi flank third-placed Jeremy McWilliams.

CHAPTER 05

BIG–
TIME
BEGINNER

Riding fast enough to race competitively at any level is a matter of feeling, and feelings are instinctive. That's why changing one's way of riding is so difficult: learning a different technique runs counter to a rider's intuition. Some riders, even elite Grand Prix professionals, never manage it. Others take years. Rossi took less than a full season.

→

By round 12 in Portugal on September 1, 2000, Rossi— here with crew chief Burgess—had fully grasped the size of the task ahead of him. This only increased his determination.

05

→ Rossi took his first win in motorcycle racing's top class on July 9, 2000, in the British Grand Prix at Donington Park.

↓ Meet the beast. Burgess stands alongside the fearsome Honda NSR500 while Rossi and Honda consultant Carlo Florenzano chat about something less evil. The bike would try to kill Rossi several times in preseason testing.

This fully restored his faith in himself, while also providing him with the different racing instincts needed to master racing for Honda. Founded by Soichiro "Pops" Honda, the company was the world's largest motorcycle manufacturer and the central hub of a racing empire. More than just a matter of publicity and a demonstration of engineering prowess, racing also developed new ideas and served as a forcing ground to train new engineers. Racing was vital to Honda, which in 1999 had won every rider and constructor championship in the premier class since 1994.

Honda had seen Rossi coming. Honda wanted him.

The attempts at recruiting started midway through 1999 from two directions. Multi-champion Mick Doohan, whose career had ended with injury earlier that year, was planning his own Shell-sponsored team.

At the same time, Honda Europe began courting the young Italian. It all got very serious when the factory team, run by the Honda Racing Corporation (HRC) itself, started making direct approaches.

At the Australian Grand Prix, round fourteen of sixteen, Rossi met Doohan's renowned crew chief, fellow Australian Jeremy Burgess. Along with his tight-knit crew, Burgess had been at a loose end since Doohan's crash. Famously matter-of-fact, he had escorted Wayne Gardner to one 500cc World Championship and then Doohan to five more. Now he showed Rossi around the class-leading V-4 Honda NSR and sounded him out on his racing credo. Both were impressed.

The deal was done two races later in Brazil, where Rossi secured the 250 crown. It was for less money than he'd been offered to stay in 250s with Aprilia, but "I knew it was what I needed to do."

↑
Rossi and the gang had plenty to laugh about at pre-season testing at Phillip Island.

←
Rossi and Jeremy Burgess prepare for a preseason test. They had no way of knowing how they would dominate the next two decades of motorcycle racing's premier class, but the looks on their faces indicate that they sensed they were on to something great.

→

Australian Mick Doohan, who had won five consecutive 500cc titles before a career-ending crash in 1999, brought Rossi into the Honda family and gifted the Italian with his brilliant crew chief Burgess, who had been instrumental in Doohan's domination of the class.

→→

Burgess and Rossi prepare for the young Italian to break his cherry in the premier class at the South African Grand Prix on March 19, 2000.

↓

Rossi's first race in the 500cc class would end inauspiciously, with Rossi losing the front end and crashing out.

He was to be in a privileged position. Sponsored by Repsol, the main factory team fielded defending champion Alex Criville, Japanese hope Tady Okada, and Spaniard Sete Gibernau. Rossi was also backed by the factory, but in an independent, one-man outfit staffed by Burgess and his boys, sponsored by Nastro Azzurro, and in his favorite yellow livery.

A 500cc Grand Prix motorcycle was different from anything Rossi had encountered so far in his career. To be blunt, he found it a real handful. The massively overpowered motorcycle lacked any of the electronic rider aids that are now taken for granted, and it was a two-stroke. This made it relatively light, with a throttle response quite a long way on the wrong side of snappish. Get your timing wrong, or give it a fraction too much gas, and it would spin the rear wheel and spit you off over the high side.

That's what happened a number of times to Rossi in the early part of the season.

There were more pitfalls. Rossi experienced another type of crash several times, when the extra weight and power scrubbed away the front wheel grip when cornering a mite too fast or leaning a mite too far, perhaps when the overworked tires had started to lose their edge after perhaps only nine or ten laps. The steering folded and the front slid away, and the rider followed the bike in a trajectory out to the gravel trap.

This was where Rossi had to unlearn his 250 riding technique and find a new way of doing things. He had to impose his will on an unwilling machine. It was a technique he had

↑
Reigning champion Alex Criville congratulates Rossi on earning his second career podium finish in the top class at the French Grand Prix. It was Rossi's second consecutive top-three..

→
Rossi wheelies to a third-place finish at Le Mans.

admired in his youth while watching heroes like Kevin Schwantz and Wayne Rainey on bikes later nicknamed "The Unrideables."

In short, it entailed treating the tarmac as if it were shale and the Grand Prix bikes as if they were flat-trackers. He'd go into the corners more slowly, turn more acutely, then open the throttle to start the back wheel spinning, at the same time picking the bike up to put the fatter part of the tire onto the track. Still only halfway round, this felt as though he would miss the corner exit and run off the track; done right (and it required courage and confidence), the spin would turn the bike, and the surge of power would precipitate him down the following straight with extra speed and momentum.

Rossi had won championships in 125 and 250 with his fast corner-speed technique,

with smooth, sweeping lines, though he added a touch of the pick-up-and-spin with the 250. Now he had to forget all of his instinctive responses and learn anew. By the end of the year, he had done well enough to win two races and finish second in the championship to Kenny Roberts Jr. on the Suzuki.

To be honest, he did have a head start: his own combination of recreation and training in the old quarry was on motocross bikes, where the same technique applies, albeit at much slower speeds.

Rossi, looking back a few years later, didn't view himself as especially skillful (a view his beaten rivals would dispute), but he thought it was his willingness to try harder that counted. At Germany's very narrow and technical Sachsenring circuit,

↗
Loris Capirossi, Rossi, and Alex Barros call a halt to the Dutch TT at Assen because of dangerous conditions.

←
Burgess and Rossi consider set-up options for the Catalonian GP on June 11, 2009. He would earn a third top three result; the Montmelo circuit would become a favorite.

where overtaking is notoriously difficult, Rossi went from sixteenth on lap one to dispute the lead (he missed the win by just eight hundredths). Having never been a good starter, he explained, "I am very used to coming from the back." The many overtakes were "not because I am better than the other guys, just because I try. Many riders say it is hard to overtake there. But if you try, maybe it's not very hard."

But it's supposed to be hard, especially in your first year on a fearsome 500. Had Rossi not been paying attention?

He'd already hit the ground several times in tests before the start of the sixteen-round season at Welkom in South Africa, where he was chasing the front group when he slid off after losing the front wheel. The same thing happened in Malaysia. And, again, he dropped to a lonely (and,

to the average class rookie, quite normal) run to eleventh at Suzuka in Japan.

Results picked up soon after: he took third at the next two races in Spain and France, then made another front-row start the next time out.

This was a big one: it was his home Grand Prix at Mugello, and the first confrontation with his rival for the hearts and minds of the ever-demonstrative fans. The swaths of Rossi yellow on the Tuscan hillsides clearly overwhelmed the patches of red for Roman emperor Max Biaggi. On the track? It was neck and neck: Rossi's Honda and Biaggi's Yamaha traded blows as they fought for the lead.

The race ended in a draw, but Rossi had blinked first, resulting in another front-end crash. Biaggi lasted a little longer before also falling.

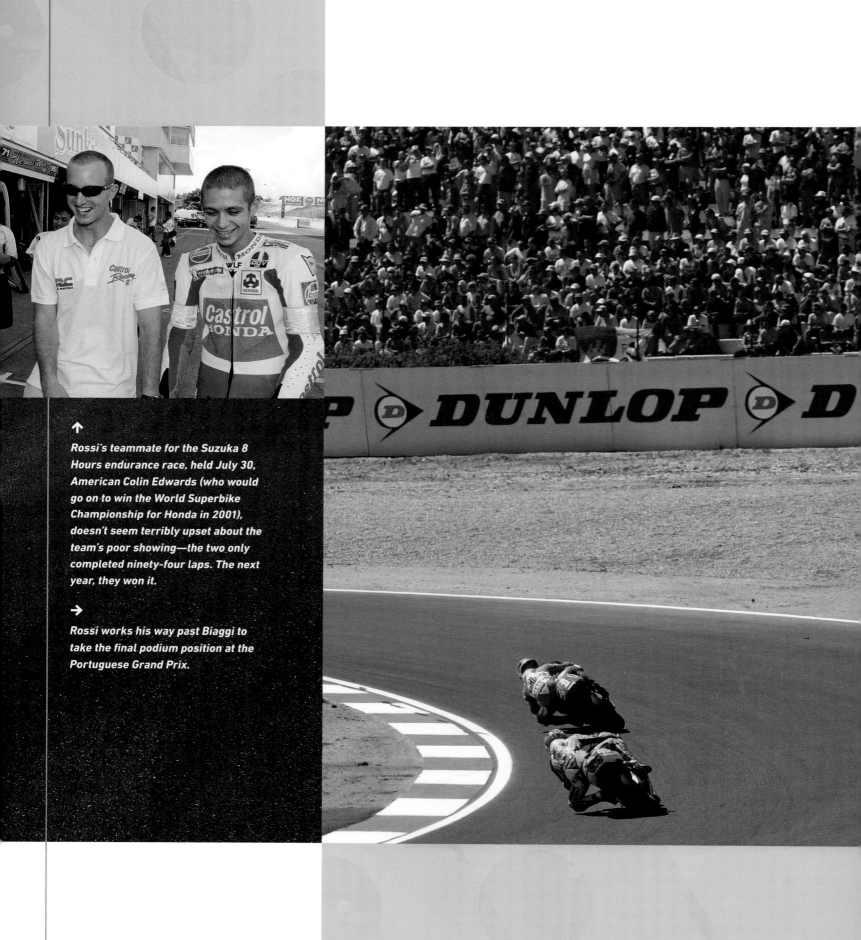

↑

Rossi's teammate for the Suzuka 8 Hours endurance race, held July 30, American Colin Edwards (who would go on to win the World Superbike Championship for Honda in 2001), doesn't seem terribly upset about the team's poor showing—the two only completed ninety-four laps. The next year, they won it.

→

Rossi works his way past Biaggi to take the final podium position at the Portuguese Grand Prix.

This battle was a key point for both riders; they had seldom come into such close contact on the track. At the penultimate round at Motegi in Japan the young upstart beat Max by less than two-tenths—although that time it was for second place.

Rossi's greater task was to adapt his riding. He'd already claimed a classic first-season win on a wet Donington Park circuit in Britain, after a thrillingly close race with eventual champion Kenny Roberts Jr. and Briton Jeremy McWilliams.

The real breakthrough, when he felt he'd fully mastered the crucial and daunting point-and-squirt technique, came at his second win of the year, at Rio.

Rossi had now firmly found his place in the big time.

Correspondingly, he had also entered the big league in terms of fame and earnings. Seeking respite from each, he now moved away from Italy to London, where he could move around more freely and also enjoy tax benefits for earnings now counted in the millions. This decision would come back to bite him and his manager Badioli.

↑
Rossi clowns around with American racer Randy Mamola at the final round of the 2000 season in Australia.

←
Max Biaggi won at Brno in 2000 and Rossi was left trailing in second. His great rival's superior performance left a sour taste; the enmity would keep on growing.

CHAPTER 06

THE LEGEND BEGINS

With Rossi's maiden dry-weather win at Rio in 2000, underlined by his rapidly growing strength in his first premier-class season, it was obvious that motorcycle racing was at the dawn of a new era. Nobody, not even Rossi, could have imagined for how long it would last or how far it could extend.

Rossi would be the last ever two-stroke 500-cc champion.

↗
For 2001 Rossi raced with Repsol livery and a new teammate, Tohru Ukawa.

→
Rossi dominated the final year of two-stroke racing in the premier class, securing the title here in Australia with win number nine.

← "P1" would be a familiar message on Rossi's pit board.

↓ Rossi won all but five races in the 2001 season.

He wasted no time in putting his name up among the greatest.

Only three riders in history had won big-bike titles on different makes of machine: Geoff Duke (Norton, Gilera) back in the 1950s, and Giacomo Agostini (MV Augusta, Yamaha) and Eddie Lawson (Yamaha, Honda) in the 1980s. Only the American, Lawson, had done so consecutively.

Rossi didn't win his first two consecutive premier-class titles on different makes. But he *did* end up winning—on two completely different motorcycles.

The first, in 2001, was on a 500cc V-4 two-stroke. The next year, he won the first MotoGP title on a 990cc V-5 four-stroke.

Apart from the name on the tank—Honda—the machines could hardly have been more different.

In his second year with Honda, Rossi gelled with the bike and with his team. Burgess observed how he had gone from a teenager to an adult during his first season . . . but he still had the same daily racetrack duty: to wake Rossi, then make sure he was up and about for first practice, because Rossi remained as dedicated as all teenagers are to staying asleep.

He marked his own progress with a new and final nickname, which he explained came to him when he had heard a Doctor Rossi being paged in an airport. Doctor is

→

Two legends whose fame transcended the sport. Barry Sheene takes a back seat to his successor, Valentino.

a mark of learning in Italy, while Rossi is a common name. He thought the two went well together so, from 2001 on, he became "The Doctor."

His championship was a bitter battle with Biaggi, but Rossi had the upper hand from the beginning, winning the first three races in Japan, South Africa, and Spain, the latter two from pole position. The first was Honda's 500th Grand Prix win, earning him special kudos with the company.

He won twice more in the first half of the sixteen-race season, but a crash and zero points at home in Italy, then a down-table seventh in round nine in Germany, meant that his more consistent Yamaha-mounted rival closed to within just ten points.

The rivalry had come close to the boiling point with a scuffle out of sight of the cameras after his fourth win in Catalonia. "A mosquito bit me," Biaggi explained when a spot of blood was noticed on his face, but he later claimed that Rossi had hit him while his own arms were pinioned. All the same, Rossi's charm won the day with the fans. They officially shook hands and made up at the next race, but it was only for the cameras. For each, the rivalry had gone up an octave.

Rossi continued to gain momentum in his second big-bike season. A confrontation at the next round at Brno in the Czech Republic saw him push Biaggi without mercy until the older rider crashed. Rossi

Rossi and Burgess proved an unbeatable combination in 2001. And in 2002, 2003, 2004, 2005, 2008, and 2009.

←

Biaggi won three of the five that Rossi didn't win in 2001.

There was little doubt as to who would win the 2001 championship.

By the time the 500 two-stroke era ended, Rossi had mastered the art of riding the most difficult motorcycles ever made.

won there, then five more times. Eleven victories put him one short of Mick Doohan's 1997 record—one that would remain forever just out of reach.

His first title was a landmark. And it was the first of many.

Rossi's improvement had been extraordinary, with six pole positions and nine fastest laps, five of them new records. It was, he said, partly thanks to the strength of his rivals, Biaggi and Loris Capirossi:

The bike is better, but especially better is me. This is normal, with more experience and kilometers. For the lap times, the battle between the three Italians was very important. If it was only two, or just one alone, it would not be necessary to go fast like this. We changed the rhythm . . . but the others were not able to.

Rossi also had a second stab at the prestigious Suzuka 8 Hours race, again partnered with American Superbike star Colin Edwards. The year before, they'd crashed out; this time, they won.

Momentous world events during the season had put completing the calendar in question following the terrorist attacks on September 11, 2001. Racing paid tribute, and then—in the way of these things—retreated into its own world again.

←

The consummate practical joker occasionally received a dose of his own medicine. Randy Mamola celebrates Rossi's first premier-class crown with a custard pie.

That world was facing a major upheaval as well: the old 500 class was to be abandoned in favor of 990cc four-strokes. And Honda had built a clever five-cylinder contender in a quest for the first honors.

Rossi rode the first version after the 8 Hours—and hated it. For one thing, it was much too small for his lanky, nearly six-foot frame. Gradually, Honda addressed his complaints with later versions, while he at first insisted on racing his beloved two-stroke NSR instead. But the much greater power of the four-stroke swung the balance. Over time, the V-5, 990cc RC211V displaced the NSR as his all-time favorite race bike.

There were a number of riders on 500cc two-strokes in 2002, including several high-level Honda men, such as Loris Capirossi. They competed at circuits where top speed was less important—Assen in the Netherlands is a prime example—and they could pose a strong challenge. But the sheer speed of the clumsier four-strokes meant it was a losing battle for the 500s. As the year began, Capirossi opined that Rossi could win the championship with one hand tied behind his back. "Not if it's my throttle hand," he responded, always ready with the right sound bite.

The two-strokes didn't win a single race; Rossi gave them little chance. He came

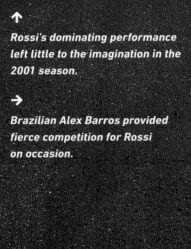

↑
Rossi's dominating performance left little to the imagination in the 2001 season.

→
Brazilian Alex Barros provided fierce competition for Rossi on occasion.

→

Having made it four out of four at the French GP, Rossi could afford to be cordial as third-place Biaggi shakes his hand. Relations would soon deteriorate sharply.

↑

In 1990, at age twenty, Alex Barros became the youngest-ever to compete in the premier class. Fifteen years later, he was still winning races.

→

Barros won one of the two races not won by Rossi or Biaggi in 2002.

out rampant to win the first race, then ten more: his second year with eleven wins. At four more, he finished second. There was only one left for the sixteen rounds: a non-finish in the Czech Republic when his rear tire disintegrated. Biaggi won it instead.

Rossi took seven pole positions until he secured the title at round twelve, and he was on the front row everywhere else up to that point. Oh yes, and he made nine fastest race laps, all but one a new record.

It sounds easy, and several times it looked easy. But that was as much a mark of his quality and dedication to victory as anything else. He was still prepared to fight when he had to, and his battle with two-race-winner Alex Barros at Assen—the Brazilian on a nimble 500 two-stroke—was memorable.

Crew chief Burgess explained to me at the end of the year how, unlike his previous multi-winner Doohan, who would basically ride the wheels off what he was given, Rossi was always looking for more from the machine. "It was common to make changes on race morning warmup, and if he liked it to change a bit more for the race."

His closest title rival was again Biaggi on the Yamaha, but this time Rossi was a massive 140 points clear. This fell short of Doohan's record margin of 143, set in 1994 and 1997. Rossi would have to wait until 2005 before he broke that record.

↓
Rossi was riding high in 2002; Sete Gibernau (left) struggled on the outpaced Suzuki four-stroke. Next year, however, the Spaniard would run him closer after joining Honda.

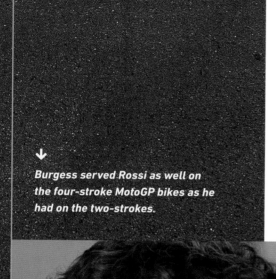

Rossi and Honda's new V-5 were on top of the world. He finished the 2002 season on the highest note possible, with his fan base and earnings growing exponentially, his results remarkable, his relationship with crew chief Burgess cemented by success, his work ethic paying off, his play ethic likewise, and a new house on the holiday island of Ibiza to add to his tax-friendly London apartment.

Yet the seeds of dissatisfaction were there. When Yamaha's race team coordinator Davide Brivio came calling to Ibiza in January of 2003, he found Rossi open minded and ready for something new.

There was another year of his current Honda contract to discharge, and another year of racing—during which Rossi maintained his momentum, winning the first race and eight more to secure his third successive premier crown on round fourteen of sixteen in Malaysia. But this time it was a bit different, and a bit harder—thanks to Honda. Anxious to prove it was their bike rather than their star rider doing the winning, they provided the latest version of the mighty V-5 to ex-Suzuki race-winner Sete Gibernau as well as to Rossi's deadly rival, Max Biaggi, who had been dumped from Yamaha. US Superbike champion Nicky Hayden joined him on the factory team.

↓

Burgess served Rossi as well on the four-stroke MotoGP bikes as he had on the two-strokes.

Although he was still on the same team in 2002, Rossi had won back-to-back championships on two completely different motorcycles.

Rossi won the first-ever MotoGP class championship in 2002.

→ *Factory Honda teammate Ukawa joined Rossi on the podium seven times in 2002, and got drenched every time.*

↓ *For one year only, two-strokes were allowed to compete alongside the four-strokes. Barros performed well on occasion, but Rossi dominated the season, winning eleven races, finishing second in four races, and not finishing one race.*

↖

Biaggi's Yamaha leads the Hondas of Rossi and the ill-fated 250 champion Daijiro Kato. Max would win just two races in 2002.

Honda's decision had been half right, for Gibernau challenged strongly at first, winning two of the first four races. He added two more, Biaggi another two. Hondas won all but one race, when Capirossi and the new Ducati took advantage of a track runoff by Rossi, who rejoined to finish second.

Honda also played hardball in its negotiations to renew Rossi's contract, underlining the belief that individual riders were dispensable. This cast his own desire for a change in high relief.

Rossi explored an option to join Ducati as well, but he found a friendlier atmosphere at Yamaha, in spite of their very

Japanese reluctance to "steal" a rider from Honda. The weight of the decision bore down heavily.

Rossi met new race department chief Masao Furusawa midseason, sneaked into the Yamaha pit at the British Grand Prix to try the bike for size, gave his handshake in a hilarious secret meeting (at one point hiding under the table) at the Czech Brno circuit, and inked a new contract after winning the title for Honda.

This turned the world of racing upside down, and it had another effect on Rossi: with Honda banning him from testing the Yamaha until the start of the year, he could enjoy a three-month holiday.

CHAPTER 07

VR46: THE STYLE OF A SUPERSTAR

There has surely never been a racer in history who owns a color like Valentino Rossi owns yellow. He's never given any special reason for the choice, just that it's bright and contrasts with pretty much everything else around. Also, he's been wearing it from his earliest racing days.

The Doctor: Rossi's cartoon image adorns his 2014 pit signaling board; his leathers look on.

A couple of years later, the scar hardly shows. Breaking his leg was Valentino's only serious injury in two decades of Grand Prix racing.

British fans made a giant Get Well card for Valentino, two weeks after he'd broken his leg in Italy in 2010. It worked. He did.

Style-conscious Rossi not only has a hand in designing his stickers, he likes to put them on the bikes himself. This Rossifumi tag dates back to 1998.

"Bright and in contrast" could be the mantra for a rider whose personality has turned natural admiration for a genius level of racing ability into a cult that spans the world. Go to any racetrack and you will see seas of yellow-clad fans, sporting their Rossi caps, shirts, and flags, screaming their adoration loud enough to drown out the constant ringing of the cash registers of his VR46 merchandising empire.

Remarkably enough, Rossi has achieved all this without artifice or cynicism. Yes, he and his advisers have made good business decisions to maximize his brand value. It all came about quite naturally, though. His popularity among the close-knit group he calls "my tribe" predates his racing success. His constant ally, Alessio "Uccio" Salucci, has been his best friend since they were at nursery school together. His fan club is run by another close friend, Flavio Fratesi, with the assistance of Uccio's father, Reno. While it only became official in 1995, Rossi acknowledges the club's formation several years earlier, when a pack of Tavullia friends and allies came to Misano to see his first race on a big bike.

His style also comes naturally. Design is something he takes seriously—from the decoration on his helmet, and the style of his leathers to (as far as sponsorship permits) the color scheme of his motorcycle. Even when there is no room to move on this, he remains fussy about the details. He supervises the placement of stickers on his bikes, even affixing them himself. He has a habit of visiting his pit late at night to commune with his machine.

This professionalism doesn't happen by accident: from his earliest Grand Prix days, he has worked hand in glove with designer Aldo Drudi, one of those figures responsible for bringing color into racing in the 1970s. In fact, Drudi had designed helmets and liveries for, among others, Kevin Schwantz.

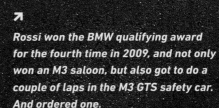

↗
Rossi won the BMW qualifying award for the fourth time in 2009, and not only won an M3 saloon, but also got to do a couple of laps in the M3 GTS safety car. And ordered one.

←
On the grid in sunny South Africa in 2002, Rossi consults with his legendary crew chief, Jerry Burgess.

With Rossi, Drudi found someone willing to experiment and be different, fed by a strong sense of style all his own. Over the years, rider and designer worked together on his regular helmet designs (updated annually, in the interests of promoting sales of replicas for helmet maker AGV) as well as on special one-off designs, most particularly for the Italian Grand Prix at Mugello.

These are eagerly awaited by fans, and they're often very witty. One of the best examples came in 2008, with a depiction of Rossi's own face with terrified, wide-open eyes and a tongue hanging out. "It shows my face when I am braking at the end of the straight here," he explained.

Other landmark designs run from the hippy "VALENTINI PEACE&LOVE" turquoise swirls of 1999 to cartoons depicting his life and his heroes (including Steve McQueen and Jim Morrison) in 2006. In 2015, they unveiled a helmet with a mirror finish "to reflect the fans at Mugello."

Others are self-parodying, like the faux-wooden finish of 2004, after a string of fourth places—to an Italian, wood comes below gold, silver, and bronze. Or, in 2005, he displayed a helmet featuring a painted-on mortarboard with the legend "Il Laureate" (The Graduate) after receiving an honorary doctorate from the University of Urbino (an award, incidentally, that irked some academics, but was very appropriate, being a doctorate in "Communications and Advertising for Organizations").

Another was touching: worn at Misano in honor of his close friend, Marco Simoncelli, who had been killed in a racing crash in Malaysia in 2013. The design was based on the Pink Floyd song "Wish You Were Here."

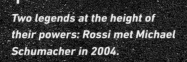

 Two legends at the height of their powers: Rossi met Michael Schumacher in 2004.

→ *Yellow, but not mellow: This is Valentino's 1997 125, with his trademark Rossifumi decals in place.*

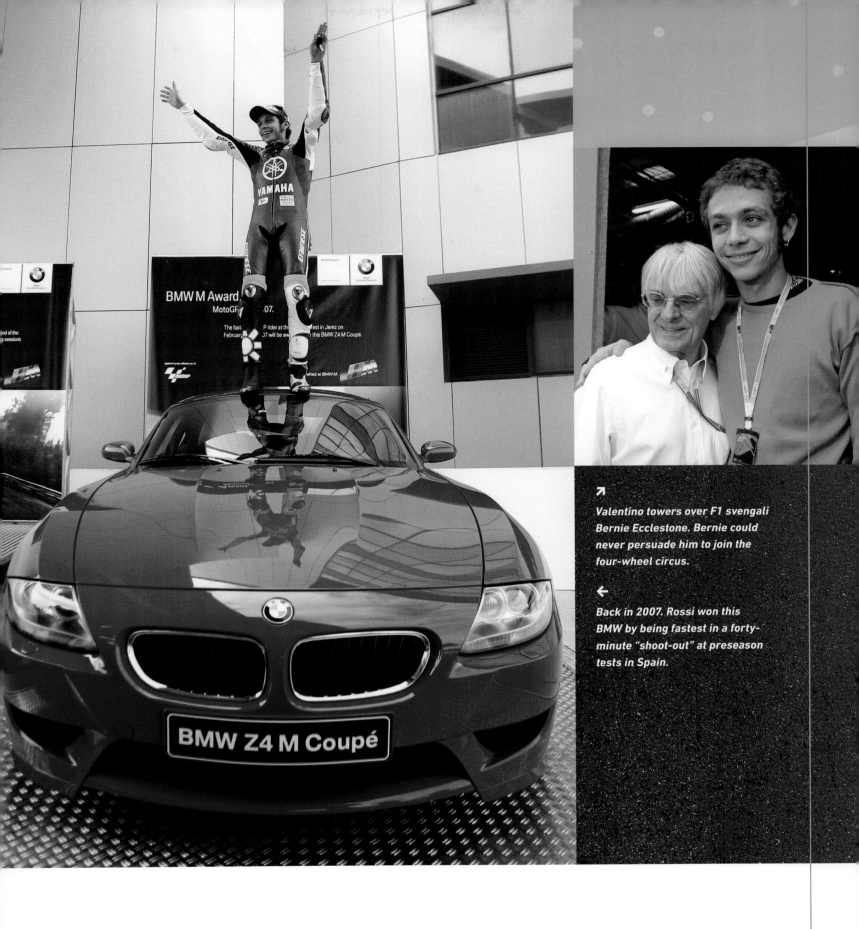

Valentino towers over F1 svengali Bernie Ecclestone. Bernie could never persuade him to join the four-wheel circus.

Back in 2007. Rossi won this BMW by being fastest in a forty-minute "shoot-out" at preseason tests in Spain.

BMW Z4 M Coupé

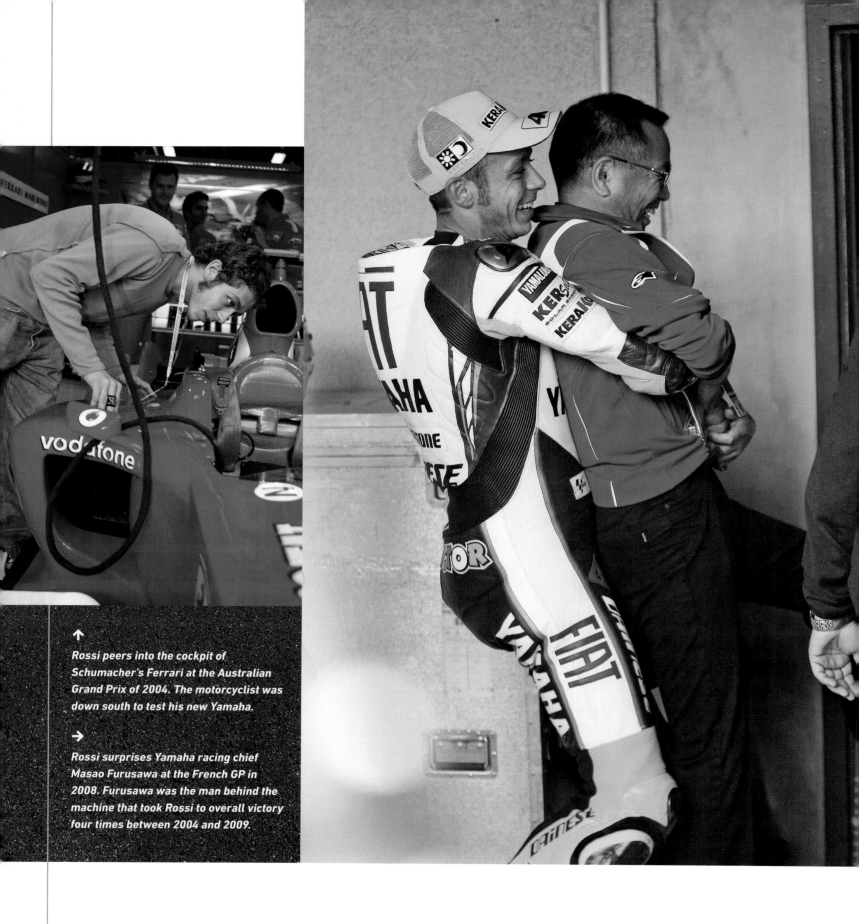

↑
Rossi peers into the cockpit of Schumacher's Ferrari at the Australian Grand Prix of 2004. The motorcyclist was down south to test his new Yamaha.

→
Rossi surprises Yamaha racing chief Masao Furusawa at the French GP in 2008. Furusawa was the man behind the machine that took Rossi to overall victory four times between 2004 and 2009.

It all started with his distinctive helmet, with sun-and-moon motifs, "reflecting," said Rossi, "both sides of my personality": the friendly, sunny side that prevails most of the time, and the dark, ruthless side when he is on the racetrack.

The same motif has evolved over more than twenty years, a fixture in his racing apparel's design.

Rossi's showmanship dates back to his schooldays, but perhaps it began in earnest in his second Grand Prix year, when he ditched the long-hair look of 1996 and started to play with different hair dyes.

Then came the postrace victory shows. And the well-chosen nicknames: Rossifumi, Valentinik, and finally, in 2001, The Doctor.

At the same time, Rossi started to understand that it wasn't all just prankish fun, and that the world wouldn't necessarily judge him on his own terms.

In his autobiography, he wrote that, in 1998, "There were too many people around who only stayed with me because I was Valentino. I thought I had more friends than I actually did."

The realization was an important step to making a business out of his image. At the same time, Dorna, the motorcycle Grand Prix rights leaseholders, had started to get organized in matters of merchandising, especially clothing—cracking down on pirate suppliers and taking control of on-track sales of rider-dedicated T-shirts, caps, and other memorabilia.

At first, Valentino's fan club concentrated only on its own range dedicated to the rider—everything from T-shirts, coats, and caps to keyrings and flags, even a stuffed turtle (like the one tattooed on his tummy) with the number 46. Replica helmets came soon, later joined by

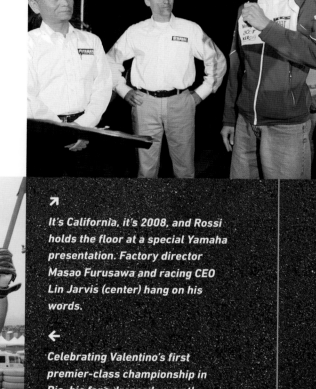

↗
It's California, it's 2008, and Rossi holds the floor at a special Yamaha presentation. Factory director Masao Furusawa and racing CEO Lin Jarvis (center) hang on his words.

←
Celebrating Valentino's first premier-class championship in Rio, his fans dressed up as the Brazilian football team.

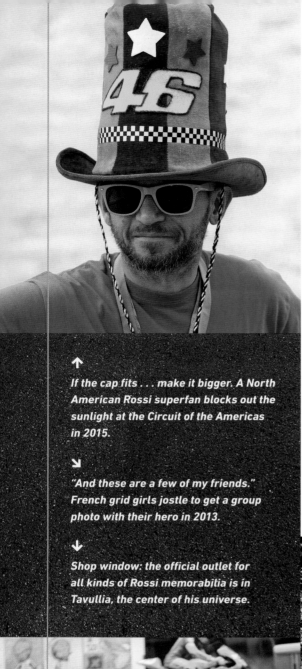

↑
If the cap fits . . . make it bigger. A North American Rossi superfan blocks out the sunlight at the Circuit of the Americas in 2015.

↘
"And these are a few of my friends." French grid girls jostle to get a group photo with their hero in 2013.

↓
Shop window: the official outlet for all kinds of Rossi memorabilia is in Tavullia, the center of his universe.

watches, cups, backpacks . . . a growing list of Rossi-brand paraphernalia.

As the organization grew in scale and efficiency, Rossi and his associates could see greater opportunities: providing the same service for other riders and taking a share of the profits.

The VR46 Racing Apparel marketing organization, based (of course) in Tavullia, was founded formally in 2012. Five years later, it employed more than thirty people, handling everything from design and production to worldwide marketing and distribution, and boasting a network covering "90 percent of countries."

The client list of twenty-five riders included MotoGP stars Dani Pedrosa, Cal Crutchlow, Pol Espargaro, Jack Miller, Scott Redding, and Rossi's 2017 teammate/rival Maverick Viñales, as well as his childhood hero, Kevin Schwantz.

One notable name was missing: that of Honda's triple champion Marc Marquez. VR46 had handled the Spanish star's range of memorabilia and merchandise until the beginning of 2016, when his contract was abruptly terminated. This was part of the fallout from the notorious confrontation between the two riders at the Malaysian GP at the end of the previous season.

The VR46 brand makes only part of Rossi's earnings, with the majority coming from product endorsements and his fee as a rider. Back in 2005, he had already made it into the top twenty of top-earning sportsmen; seven years later, the same source estimated his earnings at $30 million per year. This put him streets ahead of any other motorcycle racer, with a retail value on par with Formula 1 drivers.

Rossi's net worth was estimated at $135 million in 2017 by Sports Maza. In addition to his house and training ranch in Tavullia, he owns a luxurious holiday house in Ibiza, a magnificent Pershing 56 motor yacht, and a collection of motorcycles and cars, including a Ferrari 458 Italia. Registered "EC 046VR," it is, of course, painted bright yellow.

↑
Each a giant, and each a fan of the other. F1 champion Lewis Hamilton came to visit Valentino at Le Mans in 2013.

←
Small screen, big stars: Rossi and teammate Jorge Lorenzo fill the frame of the TV camera's viewfinder in Australia in 2009.

CHAPTER 08

ROSSI PROVES HIS POINT

Winning for Yamaha at his first attempt in South Africa was a crucial affirmation for Rossi. He had risked everything in quitting Honda for the MotoGP underdog, and, in persuading crew chief Burgess and almost the entire pit crew to come with him, they had risked everything for him.

→

Three, two, one . . . contact. This is the last corner at Jerez in 2005, and in a few yards Rossi will bump Gibernau for victory in one of the defining moments of his career.

↑

In his second Yamaha year, Rossi's former 8 Hours teammate Colin Edwards joined him.

→

Yamaha celebrated the new pairing with typical fanfare.

← Rossi brought his crew chief, Jeremy Burgess, with him to Yamaha.

↓ In 2004 Rossi did what few riders had ever dared do before: leave a winning team for a losing team.

The dream came true, albeit intermittently, over sixteen races. Rider and crew won their fourth successive championship in Australia, with one round to spare. Now he really had equalled Eddie Lawson's record, winning back to back on different makes.

But it was far from easy; at year's end, I wrote: "Nobody can now believe that he takes racing as lightly as he once might have liked to pretend."

It was hard enough adapting to a different bike, and getting it adapted to him. The biggest drawback was a lack of top speed, up against the Honda (and Ducati) opposition.

Burgess felt this most underlined Rossi's racing quality:

You need a very, very good rider to put out of their mind the speed deficit. To a rider with less mental strength, a 10- or 12-kilometer speed deficit may blow them out of the window, but a Wayne Rainey or a Valentino Rossi type . . . he did fantastically well.

For the rider, midseason: "The Yamaha is much better for settings and adjustment. We work at every race, and it is getting better all the time. Also, we get a lot of new parts." The difference was the level of effort. "With the Honda, you had time in the race to be quiet, to think about your tires and see the race develop, then push. With this bike, you have to push all the time."

His main opponent was not Biaggi, as he'd expected, but the Spaniard Sete

Gibernau, on an independent Honda. Gibernau was in the lead on points after the first seven races. He had won only two races with a string of second places, while Rossi had won four.

Rossi had regained the advantage when they arrived at Qatar for round thirteen, the first race at the new desert circuit. It was a major turning point, and the end of hitherto friendly relations between the rivals.

On race eve, Burgess and crew had used a spinning scooter wheel to lay a line of rubber at Rossi's starting point on the dusty, slippery circuit. Burgess claimed they were just making a marker to help him run over that point repeatedly in morning warmup, to clear some of the dust. But Honda (backed by Ducati) made an official protest, and race

officials decided they were cheating, giving Rossi a patch of extra grip. He was put to the back of the grid.

He passed twelve riders into the first corner, up to fourth by lap four. But then he made a rare mistake, crashed, and was out. Gibernau won the race and closed to within ten points, with three races left.

Rossi was incensed, blaming Gibernau for everything. Before leaving Qatar for treatment of his skinned left little finger, he said: "I've been looking for an excuse not to talk to Sete. Today he gave me one." He followed it up at the next race by saying he was "a bastard and a spy," adding, "He will never win another race." If his accusations seemed unfounded, this last statement would prove entirely accurate.

Turncoats. Old rivals Rossi and Biaggi swapped machines and sponsors. The results didn't change.

Preseason hijinks in the Alps with Yamaha. Rossi's international stature was growing.

↗

Like Wayne Rainey, Rossi had an unparalleled drive to win at all costs.

←

In 2004 Rossi became the first rider since Eddie Lawson (here with Ago) to win consecutive championships on two different brands of motorcycle.

↗
"He will never win another race."
Rossi hunts down Gibernau.

→
Lawson congratulated Rossi on his
third-place finish at the 2005 US
Grand Prix.

Rossi won the next three races and made history. On a Yamaha, he was champion again. Though there were more wins to follow, this may stand as his crowning achievement.

There was still a point to prove as racing started again in 2005—at Jerez in Spain, and with a battle against Gibernau's Honda. Rossi's attack at the final hairpin is still talked about today. Gibernau was in front until Rossi arrived, admitting later he'd left his braking too late. He cannoned into the Honda; while he rebounded and made it round the corner, it sent Gibernau right off the track into the dirt. He recovered to take second, almost ten seconds down. While Gibernau rubbed his bruised shoulder and gave his rival vengeful looks on the podium, Rossi ignored him and just kept laughing.

It was the start of a remarkable run. Running unsponsored in factory colors to celebrate Yamaha's fiftieth anniversary, Rossi and the M1 owned the year. He secured the title with four races to spare, having won all but four of the first thirteen (of seventeen) races and making the podium every time. He took two more, and then relaxed with a second and a third. And Gibernau remained winless.

His nearest rival was Marco Melandri, by 147 points. This time he beat Doohan's record points margin, a record that still stood in 2017.

Truly, Rossi closed off 2005 sitting on top of the world.

The next year would be much harder, and ultimately unsuccessful. Yet, in many ways, 2006 brought out the best in him, for

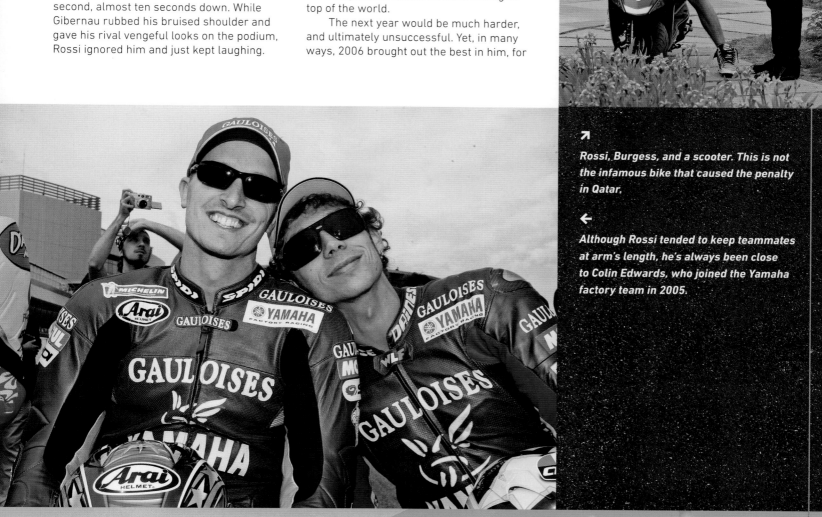

↗
Rossi, Burgess, and a scooter. This is not the infamous bike that caused the penalty in Qatar.

←
Although Rossi tended to keep teammates at arm's length, he's always been close to Colin Edwards, who joined the Yamaha factory team in 2005.

1993 World Champion Kevin Schwantz (left) was Valentino's racing hero. He copied his style, but not his high-risk temperament. Marco Melandri is on the right.

Toni Elias would beat Valentino to victory in Portugal in 2006 . . . by two thousandths of a second!

he was sporting throughout, even as he was beset by various difficulties.

It started with a narrow escape. He was knocked off at the Spanish Grand Prix's first corner by local hero Toni Elias, who almost ran over Rossi's head.

His bike touched my helmet, and I thought, "'F***, now we have another ten behind.' But the corner is slow and the other riders didn't hit me. These things happen. Toni apologized after the race, so I told him to don't worry . . . only to remember to brake next time, and if it is too late, to hit another bike instead of me."

He remounted to finish fourteenth, then won the next round in Qatar, the first of five victories, after a new chassis solved early handling problems More significant were

three zero-point races—a tire failure in China and engine blowups in France and the US. As he said later, he was beaten more by bad luck than by a better rider.

After the US race, he was fifty-one points behind American Nicky Hayden's factory Honda, with just six of seventeen rounds left. Given his continuing bike problems, he was prepared to cede victory with a smile. "I think I am happy because from now to the end for the first time I don't race with the pressure of the championship."

But there was a sting in the tail. Hayden won only two races, but his consistency meant he preserved his lead right up until the penultimate round in Portugal. There he was knocked flying by new Repsol Honda teammate Dani Pedrosa—one of the few

↑
Friends disunited. Rossi knocked Melandri down at Motegi in 2005. He took the blame, but Melandri took the injury.

←
Ex record-holder Doohan leads Mamola in a paddock scooter trail. In 2005 Rossi's 147-point defeat of Melandri outranked the Australian's widest-ever points spread.

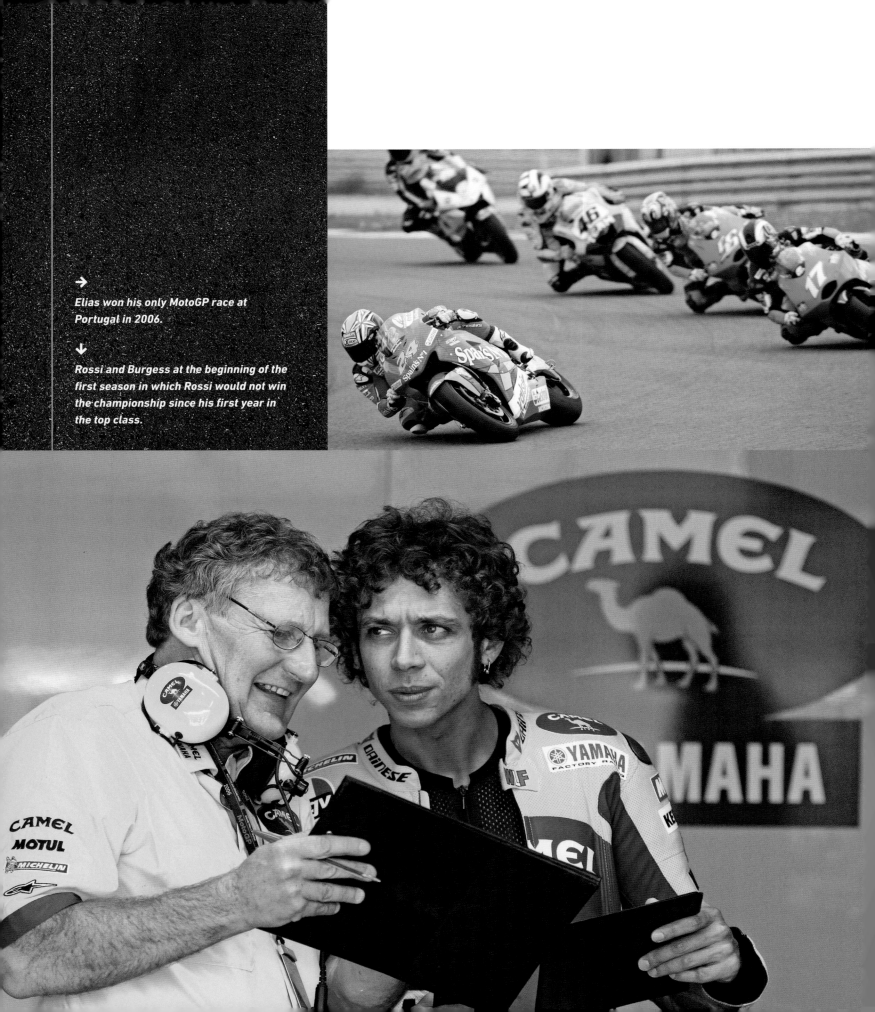

→ Elias won his only MotoGP race at Portugal in 2006.

↓ Rossi and Burgess at the beginning of the first season in which Rossi would not win the championship since his first year in the top class.

times anyone heard the popular and always polite Hayden swear.

Rossi was eight points in front for the last race at Valencia. All he needed was to follow Hayden home.

In a totally unexpected switch, however, it was Rossi who blinked in the final showdown. He crashed, remounting to finish an unlucky thirteenth. Hayden was third, the World Champion by five slender points.

A door to a different future had closed during 2006, which began rich in rumors that Rossi was going to emulate former legend John Surtees and move into Formula 1 with Ferrari. He did test the single-seater machine, but, by the sixth round in Italy, he had made up his mind. For one thing, Ferrari could only offer him practice drives for 2007. Another reason echoed what early multi-champion Geoff Duke had said: the snobbery and cold shoulder he had experienced, which Rossi described as "a bad paddock atmosphere." He added: "Formula 1 drivers are like robots. They operate under instructions from the engineers over the radio. I prefer motorcycles. When I race, I like to make my own strategy and my own decisions." Surtees's record as the only champion on two and four wheels was safe.

Rossi was still the lion of the MotoGP class, even if had been troubled by a thorn in his paw in 2006. The next year, he was a lion with a chunk taken out of its leg by a new member of the pride: young Australian Casey Stoner.

↗

While never a real competitor for the title, Toni Elias would have an impact on Rossi's 2006 season.

←

Here's a result of that impact. Track marshals help Rossi restart after Elias knocked him out of the first race of the 2006 season.

The year saw a new generation of MotoGP. The initial 990cc monsters were replaced with 800cc machines with restricted fuel capacity and a different character. This change was made with the (unsuccessful) aim of stopping the constant increase in speeds.

This time, Ducati got the technical equation right, and Stoner, blessed with massive natural talent, made the most of it. He won ten races, while Rossi won only four in his worst season so far.

There were highlights, including winning at home at Mugello and defeating Stoner at Assen by just over half second after a close race—some recompense for having been beaten by the Ducati by 0.069 of a second two races earlier in Catalonia.

But there were low moments too: crashing out in Germany, and an engine failure at home at Misano—whereupon many of the fans left before the end of the race. The final indignity was losing second overall to Dani Pedrosa in the Valencia finale. Rossi had crashed heavily in practice, returned to race with three fractures in his right hand, but he was let down again by his Yamaha. Pedrosa finished just one point ahead.

It put the cap on a dreadful year, for he was also in serious trouble with the Italian tax authorities. Seeking to make examples of famous people accused of tax evasion, they were now demanding more than 110 million euros and disputing his claimed residence in England. Their evidence included Rossi's fleet of seven

↑

Though Nicky Hayden won just two races in the 2006 season and Rossi won five, the American's consistent performance gave him the championship.

→

Rossi congratulates Hayden on his victory at the US Grand Prix.

An altercation with teammate Dani Pedrosa almost cost Hayden the 2006 championship.

Pedrosa's hairball pass initiated one of the most remarkable events in the history of the MotoGP class: Nicky Hayden using impolite language.

Italian-registered cars (a BMW M5 and M3, two Porsches, a Mercedes-Benz Sprinter, a Mini Cooper, and a Mitsubishi bus), his Pershing 50 boat moored at Gabicce Mare near Tavullia, his villa in Tavullia, and an apartment in Milan. They added the seemingly innocent fact that he had recently applied for a broadband connection in Tavullia. Rossi made a statement on Italian TV saying that he was being exploited. "The professionals who handle my income declarations have assured me that they respected the rules," he said. All the same, Gibo Badioli, the longtime manager of his London-based management company and an old family friend, was instantly dismissed.

Rossi reached an agreement with the tax department in 2008, settling for a payment of about 35 million euros. After lengthy proceedings, though, Badioli was still subject to judicial investigation, in continuing proceedings.

Could things get any worse? Perhaps . . . soon after he had pledged that he wanted "to finish my career with Yamaha," the company caused him grave offense by recruiting fast-rising Spanish star Jorge Lorenzo as his teammate in 2008. In public, he laughed about it, saying Yamaha had taken Lorenzo out of 250s "when he is too young." Privately, he was seething. He had pledged his troth to Yamaha; and here they were, hiring his replacement.

↗

Though Hayden was momentarily angry with the petite Spaniard, the American wasn't the type to hold a grudge.

←

Uneasy lies the head that wears the crown. Stoner won Ducati's first (and, so far, only) World Championship in 2007. Rossi was unable to emulate the feat.

CHAPTER 09

RIVALS

Rossi's personality is full of charm. Gracious in defeat, he is also gracious in victory— and always ready with a sound-bite quip to prove it.

→

One can't help but wonder if the bitter rivalry between Rossi and Casey Stoner motivated Rossi to join the Ducati team in 2011.

↗
Rossi's relationship with teammate Jorge Lorenzo started out friendly enough, but as Lorenzo became increasingly threatening on track, their relationship cooled.

→
Rossi's colorful character impressed as much as his incredible riding skills. Erstwhile friend Marco Melandri was a convert to colorful hairdos.

Most of the time. But there have always been certain rivals that bring out another aspect of his character, that of a ruthless killer.

This isn't surprising: nobody, in any field—let alone something as personal and risky as motorcycle racing—could achieve such massive success without being seriously addicted to winning.

He explained his feelings to me back in 2010.

First you have to understand your rival. You have to know your enemy—the good points and the bad points. You have to try to understand what your enemy thinks.

You have to hate your enemy, yes, but it depends in which way. I mean, it's possible to hate your enemy on the track but have a quite good relationship away from the track. Not a good friend, but civil.

But on the track . . . is something like what happens in the jungle, the law of the jungle. If you try to kill your enemy it's okay. If one time you don't try, for sure your enemy will kill you.

I always try to win.

His "enemy" of that the moment in 2008 was his Yamaha teammate, Jorge Lorenzo. But this was merely the latest in a long line of strong riders Rossi has used as a springboard for his own strength.

The first, and the most personal, was Max Biaggi, four-time 250 champion. Rossi and Biaggi were after a prize beyond race wins and championships; they were competing for hearts and minds (and sponsorship deals) in their native Italy. Rossi set himself against Biaggi even before they were racing in the same class: the Roman was a couple of years ahead,

→ *Biaggi ruled the 250 class while Rossi made a name for himself in the 125 class.*

and had moved to 500s when Rossi went from 125 to 250.

Biaggi had been proud and haughty, an easy target for the fun-loving teenager. While Biaggi complained about chatter (a harmonic vibration that makes fast cornering difficult) on his 500, Rossi laughingly told the Italian journalists at the circuit, "My problem [on the 250] is I don't have enough chatter. I must try to get some."

In his autobiography, Rossi admitted (surely with a cheeky grin) that he started it. "I cast the first stone."

When Rossi arrived as a Grand Prix rookie in 1996, Biaggi was riding for Aprilia and about to win his third of four successive 250 titles. He was Italy's golden boy of racing.

Not to teenage Rossi, who didn't like the way Biaggi always found someone or something other than himself to blame for problems. In his innocence, Rossi said this in an interview with an Italian journalist; the headlines were quick to promote a vendetta between the two.

This situation wasn't helped when the younger man made a further flippant remark about how, rather than hoping to be "the Biaggi of 125s, Biaggi should want to be the Rossi of 250s." Next time they met, in the circuit restaurant at Suzuka, Biaggi walked over sternly and spat, "Before you talk about me, you should wash your mouth out."

Things went downhill from there; the pair avoided one another whenever possible. Inevitably, however, they eventually met on the track. It happened in 2000: Rossi arrived in the premier class where Biaggi—now riding a factory Yamaha—had won three Grands Prix and was starting his third season on a 500.

↗
Biaggi had some success in the MotoGP class, but by then Rossi had eclipsed the Roman Emperor's star.

←
Biaggi moved up to the 500 class the same year Rossi graduated to the 250 class. The two wouldn't compete head to head until Rossi joined the top class in 2000.

OFFICIAL FAN CLUB
VALENTINO ROSSI 46

↑

Nobody in racing history has generated fan hysteria like Valentino. Here they celebrate in Catalunya, after their hero's third win of 2016.

→

The Rossi-Biaggi saga erupted in something that could charitably be described as "violence" at Suzuka in 2001.

↓

Can't win 'em all. Vale looks pensive as Biaggi celebrates victory in the Dutch TT at Assen in 2001. The race had been cut short by rain, Rossi's planned attack was over-ruled by the weather.

Tension simmered throughout that year. Then it boiled over at the first round of 2001, the Japanese Grand Prix at Suzuka, a fast and dangerous track no longer used for MotoGP.

The pair engaged in tough close combat in the early laps, and Biaggi was fractionally ahead when they emerged onto the pit straight before half distance. With Rossi almost alongside on his left, the older rider let his red Yamaha drift ever wider. At close to top speed, he pushed Rossi right off the track and onto the grass. Of course Rossi could have backed off instead, but not with Biaggi.

He regained control, set off after the Yamaha, and soon passed him round the outside on a fast right-hander, taking his left hand off the handlebar to flip him an eloquent one-finger salute as he did. Rossi came first, Biaggi third. It was Honda's 500th win.

The actions of both prompted a fulsome open letter from the president of the sanctioning federation, the FIM, exhorting them at length to show sportsmanship and respect for the dignity of the sport. Predictably, Rossi found it hilarious.

With sniping and sneering remarks in public and icy avoidance elsewhere, their enmity flourished for as long as they raced one another, famously boiling over again in a physical fight out of the public's sight on the stairs to the podium at Catalonia in 2001.

The results were heavily in Rossi's favor, with fifty-three wins between 2000

Suzuka, 2001, and Valentino uses his Honda as an impromptu podium after winning the opening round of the last 500cc two-stroke season. He went on to his first premier-class title, closing one era and opening another.

Marco Melandri had been a close friend of Rossi's prior to joining the premiere Grand Prix racing class.

↗

Hayden leads Rossi in Australia: they were Repsol Honda teammates in 2003 and together again at Ducati almost ten years later, and good friends throughout.

→

Son of a legend, Kenny Roberts Jr. took the title in Rossi's first top-class season. But here Rossi has just won his first 500 GP.

Hayden would defeat Rossi for the championship in 2006. He'd rather have lost to the American than anybody else.

Gibernau was not the psychological warrior that Rossi was, and the bitter rivalry took a toll on the Spaniard.

and 2005 compared with ten for Max. So too went popular appeal, with Biaggi's patches of red on the hillside vastly outnumbered by the Rossi fans' oceans of yellow.

Looking back after retiring from Grand Prix racing at the end of 2005, a mellower Biaggi recalled, "For me, it was a good rivalry because it helped the sport a lot. Fair or unfair? What can I say? What is fair in racing?"

Having successfully defused the multi-250 champion's threat, Rossi had others to deal with. Former teenage friend and dirt-track playmate Marco Melandri had been following a few years behind him. When he got up to speed in the 500 class, he discovered that all you needed to unravel an old friendship was to be threateningly fast.

When I started to race well with him, he changed a lot. When we were growing up, we were very good friends.

Valentino plays games with everybody . . . The way he talked to the media—he tries to never say something good about you. When he knows you can fight with him, he tries to speak always about the other riders. He wants to show you he doesn't think about you. When he does like this, he is scared about you. But he's very smart.

A greater threat came from Sete Gibernau. Rossi told me that he took the most pleasure in beating him, "always . . . because before we were quite good friends, and after we have some problem out of the track, so the enemy became bigger. The motivation."

For the defeated Spaniard, I never felt I was only racing Valentino, but it was him and myself for two or three years, battling every race. I was trying to become a better rider. I could only control what I was doing.

Rossi is a very complete rider—mentally and talent-wise. He believes a lot in himself. That is one of his big weapons.

He was never my enemy. I was never trying to be anyone's enemy. I was enjoying racing, and pushing myself. But maybe he needed me as an enemy.

At Qatar, he blamed me, but it was nothing I did. Of course I didn't report him. I didn't even see what happened. I'd had a very good relationship with Valentino for many years. But after that, it just came around.

The late Nicky Hayden, an erstwhile teammate, escaped Rossi's vengeance, even after he beat him for the championship. Having come through tough times in US dirt-tracking, he felt immune. "I don't think he played many mental games with me. If he did, it didn't faze me. Or I didn't notice it. But with Biaggi and Gibernau—I would say he broke them poor boys down."

But that was before Jorge Lorenzo arrived as his threatening teammate—and Rossi insisted on a wall dividing the Yamaha pit firmly in two.

The pair never descended to fisticuffs on the way to the podium, remaining distantly polite, by and large, in public. But they were more than just uneasy colleagues: Jorge's very presence made Rossi so disillusioned with Yamaha that it triggered his biggest career mistake ever—walking out and going to Ducati at the end of 2010.

Rossi's friendship with Marquez soured during the 2015 season.

←

Rossi and Hayden in 2003. Their relationship remained warm until the American's untimely death in 2017.

→
Rossi goes for escape velocity as he tries to outdistance his latest challenger. Honda's Marc Marquez would go on to win the 2013 championship at the first attempt.

The Ducati-Italian dream foundered; Rossi returned to Yamaha alongside Lorenzo in 2012. By 2015 he was back on form, but now there was a new kid on the block. Honda's Marc Marquez had won the title in 2013, the youngest ever, and dominated in 2014.

At first the past master and the tyro got on well. Fourteen years older, Valentino treated the former fan differently from past challengers. In their first on-track clash, in 2013's round one at Qatar, they fought throughout, Rossi ahead by barely two-tenths. Afterward, they embraced warmly. The bromance was reinforced when Marquez much upset Lorenzo, with a Rossi-style bash at the Jerez hairpin. It survived through 2014.

It couldn't last. And when it soured at the end of 2015, it was spectacular.

Marquez had a difficult third season with a hard-to-handle Honda. Rossi's Yamaha led on points when they arrived in Australia, with three races to go. He had four wins, Lorenzo six, but greater consistency put Rossi 18 points ahead.

There had been two significant on-track clashes with Marquez—physical bangs (what riders euphemistically call "touches") —in Argentina and at Assen. Both times Rossi came out on top. But now the strain was starting to show.

In Australia, Marquez pushed past Lorenzo to win, Rossi forth. He retained the lead, 296 to 285. But something had changed in his mind. Together with best friend Uccio, he pored over the lap-by-lap timings and came to a seemingly irrational conclusion. Even though Marquez had effectively robbed Lorenzo of five points by beating him, Rossi insisted on an all-Spanish conspiracy—that Marquez was trying to help Lorenzo to the title.

The numbers didn't add up, but that made no difference to Rossi, nor to his vast worldwide army of fans.

A week later in Malaysia, Rossi laid into a flabbergasted Marquez at the pre-race press conference, with implausible but vehement accusations of conspiracy.

The incident in Sunday's race was even harder to understand. While Pedrosa escaped to win, Lorenzo was a safe second—because Rossi and Marquez had slowed each other in his wake in a tit-for-tat battle more like a playground punch-up than World Championship racing. The outcome was awful.

On lap seven of 20, Rossi slowed radically, and turned to eyeball the young Spaniard. Marquez swerved round the outside, but Rossi veered ever wider. They collided. Marquez went down.

Had Rossi kicked out, fouling Marquez's front brake? This was Honda's allegation, and they promised to prove it at the final round in Valencia. Any evidence was abruptly and

PRAMAC
AUSTRALIAN
MOTORCYCLE
GRAND PRIX

Phillip Island 2015

←

The crucial podium. Winner Marquez is flanked by Jorge Lorenzo (second) and Andrea Iannone. Rossi was fourth and furious. A fortnight later in Australia, his anger erupted.

↓

Two years later, and the order is reversed. Double champion Marquez outpaces Valentino at Australia's Phillip Island. The consequences were far-reaching.

→ The smiling assassin. Marquez looks bewildered as Rossi reveals his suspicions of a Spanish conspiracy at the pre-race press conference in Malaysia in 2015.

↓ Fateful race. Early laps at Sepang, and Rossi is focused on erstwhile leader Marquez. Lorenzo, sandwiched between them, benefitted from the feud and won the race ...

←

... and two weeks later the 2015 title. Victory at Valencia's final round, with Rossi only fourth after a punishing pit-lane start, gave his Spanish team-mate his third championship by just five points.

inexplicably withdrawn on the day. By now the situation was out of hand: Rossi fans lobbed death threats to Marquez on social media, his family was physically threatened at home in Spain, bodyguards were deployed in the Valencia paddock, while the pre-event media conference was cancelled for fear of another blow-up. And Yamaha cancelled its 60th anniversary party.

Meanwhile, Race Direction had penalized Rossi with a back-of-the-grid start, and his appeal to the Court of Arbitration for Sport was declined on race eve.

He fought through to fourth, but if there'd been little evidence of a Spanish conspiracy before, that had changed. Compatriots Marquez and Pedrosa dutifully followed winner Lorenzo home, and he beat Rossi to the title by five points.

Mind games or deluded outbursts, the flaming row had cost Valentino his chance of a tenth World Championship.

CHAPTER 10

PRIDE COMES BEFORE A FALL

The 2008 season was payback for the problems of the last two: nine wins, beating Casey Stoner by close to 100 points, as Ducati development seemed to lose its way.

→

Rossi congratulates arch-rival Stoner on a hard-fought win in the 2008 German Grand Prix.

→ Rossi's bike was up to the task.

↓ After a disappointing fifth in the season opener at Qatar, Rossi finished on the podium in the next two races.

Rossi took a couple of races to get going, finishing only fifth when the first-ever night race in Qatar opened the season, but by round three in China he embarked on three wins in a row. The real purple patch came after the summer break: five straight wins in Laguna Seca, Brno, Misano, Indianapolis, and Motegi, where he secured his sixth premier-class championship with three of eighteen rounds to spare.

He also passed another landmark: beating Agostini's record of sixty-eight premier-class wins with his sixty-ninth at Indianapolis.

One crucial factor was Rossi's switch from Michelin to the Bridgestone tires Stoner was already using. One outcome was that, with his new teammate still using Michelins, a wall was made down the middle of the pit, ostensibly for each tire company to be able to keep its secrets. But there was also a ban from Rossi on letting Lorenzo see any of his data. When both were on the same Bridgestone tires in 2009, the wall stayed in place.

The atmosphere between the two was respectful enough outwardly, but the tension was plain to see.

Lorenzo notwithstanding, Rossi—now negotiating on his own behalf since the departure of Badioli—had signed up for another two years with Yamaha in the middle of 2008. He cemented his relationship with the M1 by winning the title again in 2009. It was his fourth on the Yamaha, his seventh in the premier class, and his ninth World Championship in all classes. At the time of writing, in 2017, it was also his last.

↗
Rossi began the 2008 season determined to regain the championship.

↓
Rossi took his second consecutive victory at Le Mans.

But he was already more than an international icon and a massively successful brand name in his own right: he was also racing's new History Man. He had joined Mike Hailwood and Giacomo Agostini on the notional list of Greatest of All Time. Meanwhile, another candidate, pioneering first American World Champion Kenny Roberts, had proved long before that, as long as you remain competitive, you can still be called King—even when others are taking overall honors. Rossi was set to do that for far longer than the American superstar.

The 2009 season was seventeen races long and had introduced another major change. After a tough 2007, in which previously the dominant Michelin team had gotten red faces, Bridgestone was appointed MotoGP's first "control tire" supplier. It was "one size fits all," and if Rossi was complaining about the lack of choice (just two different front and rear tires at each race), at least he acknowledged that anything making for closer racing "is good for the fans." Knowing what they meant to his career, he has always put them first.

With Stoner stricken with chronic fatigue, later diagnosed as a symptom of lactose intolerance, Rossi's acknowledged rival was now Lorenzo, who had won a race in his debut MotoGP season in 2008. The Spaniard took a narrow overall lead over the first five races, and would win four times over the year. But at round six in Catalonia, in a bitter dogfight, Rossi stamped his authority with an audacious last-corner overtake to win by less than a tenth of a second. It was his ninety-ninth Grand Prix win. His hundredth, at the next round at Assen, was a cakewalk by comparison.

↑
Rossi shares a laugh with Mick Doohan at Brno.

→
Former teammate and fellow Yamaha rider Colin Edwards shared the podium with Rossi at Le Mans.

Rossi's Le Mans victory was his 90th, putting him equal with legendary thirteen-time 50 and 125 World Champion Angel Nieto. The Spanish veteran joined him to celebrate the landmark.

↗

Rossi devises new ways to mess with Stoner's head at Brno.

→

Rossi poses with Agostini, who was watching the younger Italian pick off one of his records after another.

From there to the end, over six wins and five second places, Rossi gradually pulled clear, securing the crown with third place at a sodden Sepang in Malaysia.

Lorenzo's growing threat, and Yamaha's support for him, were now beginning to grate seriously. Rossi remained outwardly cheerful, but his words to me in an interview late in 2009 revealed the depth of his disquiet.

Having such a strong teammate was, he said . . . different. It's a different way to work in the team also. Usually the big manufacturers in the last years have always had just one top rider each. There are two of us at Yamaha, so this is a different strategy that can bring good results, but also big disasters.

On the track, it's more satisfying to win, because you are at the same level.

But usually I always try to put a lot of work in developing the bike, and I usually do it just for me. But now I'm also doing it for my worst enemy. You know . . . sincerely, I don't think I deserve this, after what I did for Yamaha. But this was Yamaha's choice.

Speaking to Italian pressmen, he confirmed his feelings. "I think Yamaha has to choose between him and me."

The writing was on the wall. With Yamaha committed to keeping Lorenzo, there wasn't anywhere else for Rossi to go except Ducati. After all, Stoner was winning races on it.

Rumors of the move started at the second round of the 2010 season, with Stoner linked to a move to Honda and Rossi to a dream all-Italian team with Ducati. Both of these came true, so when confirmation finally came at the tenth of eighteen rounds at Brno, it was no surprise. But it was stunning nonetheless. The reigning champion and international superstar Rossi was moving to the only non-Japanese team to win the championship since 1975, for a sign-on fee rumoured at fifteen million euros.

It was an all-Italian dream indeed. Even if he never drove for Ferrari, this was certainly the next best thing.

The fact that 2010 was his most difficult season in the premier class seemed almost incidental. Yes, he lost his title to teammate Lorenzo. But it was not because he'd been outridden. For the first time in his whole Grand Prix career—now spanning fifteen years—he sustained a serious injury, missing four races as Lorenzo claimed four wins in a row to make himself effectively unbeatable.

For a rider who has always seemed able to walk away from anything, the injury was painful and public. In practice for his home race at Mugello, he was caught out when his tire cooled a little too much after he'd been slowed by another rider. The heavy high-side crash left him writhing in the sand-trap, his right leg visibly distorted with a double compound fracture.

Intensive therapy and unquenchable determination meant he was out for only forty-one days, returning on crutches to Germany. This came after orthopaedic metalwork to plate and screw the injury at the Centro Traumatologico Ortopedico in

Even though Rossi had the championship in the bag with four races remaining, he raced as hard in the remaining four Grands Prix as he did all season. Here he is about to pass James Toseland in Australia.

Rossi's young friend Marco Simoncelli congratulates him on winning the 2008 championship at Motegi in Japan.

↑
Rossi celebrates winning a shortened, hurricane-hit Indianapolis Grand Prix in 2008. It was his 69th in the top class . . . one more than Agostini.

←
Rossi wheelies to victory at the Malaysian Grand Prix.

↗

Although Australian Casey Stoner took third place at Jerez in 2009, he would not prove to be the competitor he had been the previous year.

→

Rossi shared the podium with Dani Pedrosa at Jerez in 2009. The diminutive Spaniard has become a respected rival over the years.

Florence, where he had spent fifteen days lying on his back. There followed dull and uncomfortable sessions in a hyperbaric (high-pressure) chamber and training bouts of five or six hours a day. Ten days before the German race, he tested a street bike at Misano circuit, then a Yamaha Superbike at Brno, before electing to get back to his M1 as soon as possible.

The last hurdle was the German track doctor. He passed that test, proving that he had "90 percent knee movement, and 95 percent in the ankle, and I could walk. The doctor was very surprised that I was able to walk without crutches . . . the problem is that my leg can get very big if I do that." The special Dainese leathers and boot were enlarged, padded, and reinforced in the affected area. He eventually qualified fifth and finished fourth.

He was third and on the podium next time out at Laguna Seca (and vastly amused when the circuit mistakenly played the Italian national anthem instead of winner Lorenzo's Spanish tune).

With the news of his departure now public, he gleefully pursued his vendetta against Lorenzo. At the Japanese Grand Prix, where a win for the Spaniard could have tied up the title after his last challenger, Pedrosa, was injured, Rossi engaged him in nonstop, "hand-to-hand" combat, changing places six times on the last lap to secure third. Lorenzo said darkly, "He will get it back," and complained to Yamaha. Big boss Masao Furusawa called Rossi in for a cautionary chat. Rossi emerged giggling, saying, "Yamaha asked me to race with more attention. So if I am fighting again with Lorenzo, I will try to beat him again . . . with more attention."

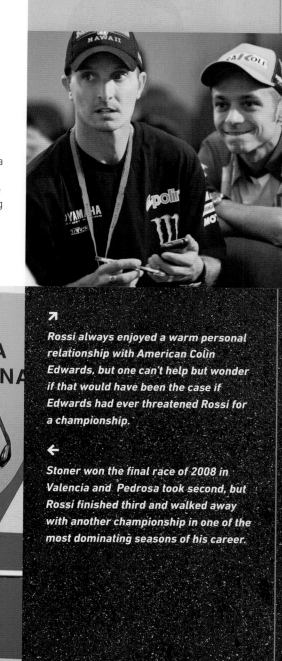

Rossi always enjoyed a warm personal relationship with American Colin Edwards, but one can't help but wonder if that would have been the case if Edwards had ever threatened Rossi for a championship.

Stoner won the final race of 2008 in Valencia and Pedrosa took second, but Rossi finished third and walked away with another championship in one of the most dominating seasons of his career.

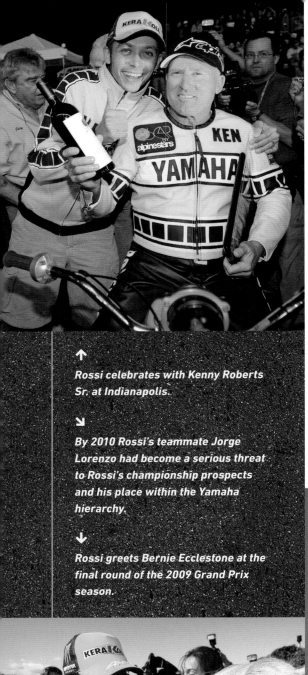

Rossi celebrates with Kenny Roberts Sr. at Indianapolis.

By 2010 Rossi's teammate Jorge Lorenzo had become a serious threat to Rossi's championship prospects and his place within the Yamaha hierarchy.

Rossi greets Bernie Ecclestone at the final round of the 2009 Grand Prix season.

"I said to Yamaha, what do you expect from me, to arrive behind? If I know this, I will stay at home."

A week later, at Sepang, Lorenzo secured the title, but Rossi poached much of the attention, taking his second win of the year. Significantly, it was Yamaha's forty-sixth class win, matching his number. "46 is good," he said. "But 47 is better."

In the final count, Rossi was third overall behind Pedrosa, but he was still the king of the class. The leg break, however, was not his most costly injury: he had injured his right shoulder—after having won the first GP of the year—in a training accident at home while riding motocross. As well as a small fracture and ligament damage, it was not dislocated but "it tried to come out." This caused him pain and weakness all year long; after the last race, he was off for corrective surgery.

Turning his back on Yamaha had been a major decision, and an emotional one as well. He expressed his feelings in a hand-written "love letter" to his motorcycle. Translated from Italian, it read:

Many things have changed since that far-off time in 2004, but especially "she," my M1, has changed. At that time she was a poor, middle-grid-position MotoGP bike, derided by most of the riders and MotoGP workers. Now, after having helped her to grow and improve, you can see her smiling in her garage, courted and admired, treated as top of the class.

Unfortunately, even the most beautiful love stories end, but they leave a lot of wonderful memories, like when my M1 and I kissed for the first time on the grass at Welkom, when she looked straight in my eyes and told me "I love you."

Would he fall in love with the proud and elegant Ducati?

Rossi rode well in 2010, but a broken leg sustained in a crash while practicing in Mugello early in the season took him off the track for four races and effectively killed his chances of winning an eighth premier-class championship.

A third-place finish at Malaysia secured Rossi's championship for 2009, with one round remaining.

CHAPTER 11

THE WILDERNESS YEARS

By now it's been said so often that it is way beyond cliché: Rossi's move to Ducati for an all-Italian dream team was nothing short of a nightmare.

→

Rossi hoped to do at Ducati what he had done at Yamaha—resume his winning ways from the start.

→ The biggest story of 2011 wouldn't be Rossi at Ducati, but the death of Rossi's close friend Marco Simoncelli.

↓ Simoncelli leads Dovizioso, Rossi, and Ben Spies. His riding style was wild ever since his 2002 debut on a 125.

A nightmare prolonged by false optimism, worsened halfway through by a ghastly accident, in which Rossi played an unwitting part in causing the death of one of his closest friends.

The crash was at Sepang in Malaysia, the seventeenth of a planned eighteen races. The fast-rising Marco Simoncelli was eight years younger than Rossi, but he was a kindred spirit, from the same part of town. They were good friends, often training—and socializing—together.

Sporting a leonine mane of hair, Simoncelli had won the 250 crown. In MotoGP, he'd earned a reputation as a wild rider as well as claiming his first podium. Now, early in the next race, a freak crash carried him back under the wheels of following riders Colin Edwards and Rossi; both ran over him. He was fatally injured.

The heartbreak came after an increasingly difficult first Ducati season.

Rossi and his crew chief Burgess had allowed themselves to be flattered into thinking that they could reverse the decline in Ducati's results.

Casey Stoner had romped to the 2007 title on the loud, very fast, vivid red Italian V-4 with ten race wins. Since then, the win rate had kept going down, with only three in 2010, interspersed with many crashes.

Rossi and his team blamed the rider. They were sure their setup and development skills could soon get the bike winning again; they were very wrong. The bleak look on their faces at the first test at Valencia, directly after the last GP of 2010, would only become more drawn as the two-year contract ran its course.

↗
Simoncelli won the 250cc World Championship in 2008. Runner-up Alvaro Bautista shakes his hand.

←
Simoncelli demonstrates his press-on style at preseason tests in Malaysia.

↗

Simoncelli passes Rossi's Ducati teammate Nicky Hayden in what would turn out to be the Italian's final race.

↓

Marlboro men. Rossi and Hayden join their four-wheel counterparts, F1 racers Fernando Alonso (left) and Felipe Massa.

Beyond the bad news on the track, surgery to Rossi's shoulder that winter had uncovered worse tendon damage than expected. It continued to trouble him for half the year.

When the season began at Qatar, Stoner, now with Honda (just to rub it in) galloped to victory from pole position. He carried on much the same to win overall. Rossi was a downbeat seventh, and he too would also carry on much the same.

Early in the year, Rossi spoke about his early impressions of the Desmosedici.

Historically, the Ducati bike has always been evil, nasty. You have to ride it with your claws. Compared with the M1 Yamaha, it must be driven with a dirtier style. But I hope to be able to make it easier for me. It's a bike. You can change whatever you want.

For my part, I'm also going to have to change my riding style to exploit this bike to the maximum. I think I will be able to do it.

He and his team did their best, as did the factory. Unique to racing bikes, the Ducati didn't have a full chassis, using the engine with a "mini-chassis" up front that doubled as the all-important induction air box. It was made of carbon fiber, not aluminum, which was the material of choice for all the other manufacturers. At this time, great advances were being made in understanding the need for controlled chassis flexibility. The Ducati's mini-chassis was much too stiff. Replacing the carbon fiber with aluminum saw no improvement: by year's end, a more conventional aluminum chassis arrived—but it made little difference.

Tribute to the fallen. Davide Brivio (left), Rossi, and a Ducati mechanic walk to the inauguration of the Simoncelli memorial in Malaysia in 2012.

→

Simoncelli's father and girlfriend were in the paddock when he crashed.

↗
Marlboro Ducati line-up in the Dolomites at the pre-season launch, with current Ducati CEO Claudio Domenicali on the left.

→
Rossi chose a recreational vehicle a bit more suitable to the climate than a MotoGP bike.

Ducati also produced a new engine—next year's 1000cc unit (the rules due to change again), reduced in capacity to 800cc. Still no breakthrough.

Meanwhile, Rossi and Stoner had clashed at the second race at Jerez; the Italian lost control and took Stoner out of the race. The Australian was memorably eloquent, going to Rossi's pit and asking, "Did you run out of talent?"

Rossi had little to say in response. "I made a mistake. I would have been more happy to crash alone. I hope Stoner never makes a mistake like that in his career." He added, with his impish grin, "I don't think he likes me very much."

Round four in France brought a false dawn, when Rossi was promoted to third by incidents ahead of him. It was his only podium of the year. His next best results were three fifth places; while he was never below tenth, his progress was defined by crashing out of the last three races of the year. Seventh overall.

Admirably, he never lost his optimism, pouring scorn on suggestions that he might bail out of his two-year contract halfway through.

But he also made his feelings clear with a special helmet design for round thirteen close to home at Misano. A cartoon thought-bubble included a bomb, lightning bolts, exclamation marks, a black cat, and a skull-and-crossbones. "It is what I am thinking when I am riding. I tried to explain it without words . . . because if I had a helmet just with the word 'F*CK' on it, it wouldn't be polite."

For 2012, the 1000cc MotoGP bikes were back, and Ducati acquired a more

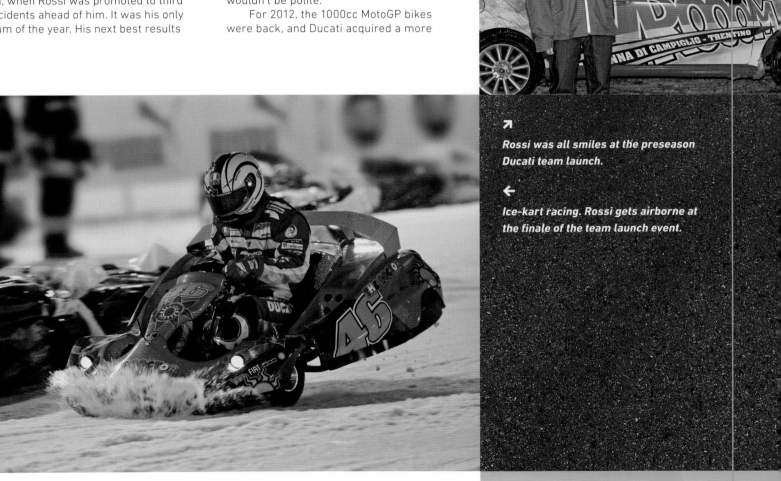

↗
Rossi was all smiles at the preseason Ducati team launch.

←
Ice-kart racing. Rossi gets airborne at the finale of the team launch event.

→ *The initial celebrations of Rossi's arrival at Ducati would prove to be the high point of his time there.*

↓ *Rossi's famous smile would become increasingly strained during his two years with Ducati.*

conventional aluminum chassis. Rossi finished one place higher in the championship and twice on the podium. But there was no real progress, or at least nothing soon enough to convince him to stay. He was equally unimpressed after the Italian company was acquired midyear by the Audi Group, part of the giant Volkswagen empire. The new owners' blandishments, aimed at getting Rossi to sign up again, were rumored to include a massive 15-million-euro offer.

The year started badly at Qatar, where he qualified a dismal twelfth, managing only to move up to tenth in the race. His comments were now becoming more strained. "Everyone in MotoGP is very fast, so it's very easy to go in the back."

By the next race, there were already rumors that he was approaching Yamaha,

while Honda team chief Shuhei Nakamoto made it clear there was no way back to Honda. Referring to Rossi's autobiography, *What If I Had Never Tried It*—in which he argued it was the rider, not the bike that mattered—Nakamoto said, "Now it is time for him to prove it."

His first time on the podium over eighteen rounds was in the rain at Le Mans, where his riding skills in difficult conditions meant more than the GP12 Ducati's persistent lack of balance. "Any time you wish for rain, you are in shit," he laughed after the race.

At that same weekend, round four, reigning champion Stoner revealed he was to retire at the end of the year, taking all concerned by surprise. Rossi was asked if he might follow suit. "No. I never think to stop," he said. "I like the racing life a lot, the weekend of the GP. To stop at the top is the

↖

Rossi brought Stoner down at the Spanish GP, but remounted to finish fifth. After the race Stoner accused him of "running out of talent."

←

It became apparent in preseason testing that turning the 2011 Ducati into a race winner was no easy task.

↗

Rossi crashed out of the Japanese GP at Motegi on October 2, 2011.

→

Two weeks later he crashed out of the race at Phillip Island in Australia.

dream of every sportsman, but for me the price is too high."

The mid- to low-end top-ten results continued, plus a dismal thirteenth at Assen. Soon after came the summer break . . . and the announcement everyone had been expecting with growing confidence.

Rossi was going back to Yamaha, rejoining Jorge Lorenzo. But now the Spaniard was the chosen one, Rossi just an afterthought.

His move would mean a significant pay cut, as Yamaha Racing chief Lin Jarvis explained: "Honda made maximum effort to secure Lorenzo, and he has been taken care of very well . . . so for Valentino there is not a huge budget remaining." There was no "number one rider," as such, but: "We consider Jorge the most capable to win the World Championship," said Jarvis. Project manager Kouichi Tsuji added, "In develop-

ment, Lorenzo will decide the direction for the bike . . . he will lead, but Valentino will assist."

It would be a major step down, but then it would be up to Rossi to see what he could do about it.

He celebrated with a second podium finish at his local San Marino circuit, partly thanks to extensive prerace practice.

Rossi left a confused Ducati behind him, where longtime design guru Filippo Preziosi paid the price for two years of failure, being forced to another part of the company to make way for a German Audi nominee.

All the same, it would take several years before Ducati could again threaten the results that Preziosi and Stoner had achieved before the Rossi misadventure.

By now, many were writing Rossi off as a spent force.

↗

The more Rossi tried to overcome his handling problems, the more he crashed the Ducati. This is in practice at Catalonia.

↓

Rossi ended the worst racing season (and worst year) of his life by getting caught up in a multi-bike crash at Valencia.

CHAPTER 12

THE RETURN OF THE NATIVE

Rossi had swallowed his pride and rejoined Yamaha as junior partner to Jorge Lorenzo. Simultaneously Old Master and Work In Progress, the great hero's return from the Ducati doldrums went to plan in almost every respect except one: the timescale.

→

On the podium in Texas. With just three races to go, Rossi arrived in Australia leading the 2015 Championship.

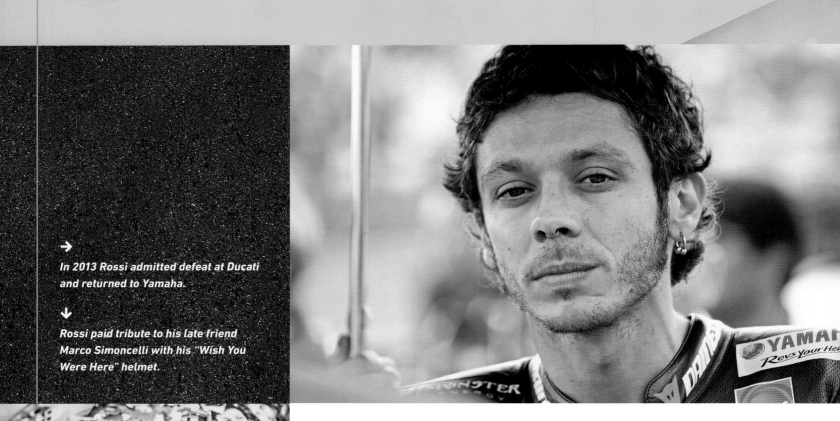

→

In 2013 Rossi admitted defeat at Ducati and returned to Yamaha.

↓

Rossi paid tribute to his late friend Marco Simoncelli with his "Wish You Were Here" helmet.

He'd eaten humble pie, figuratively and financially. The figures remain secret, but it was rumored his fee had more than halved, in the region of five million euros, while Lorenzo—who was being courted by Honda—was to be paid considerably more than double that.

Rossi had left Yamaha because he wasn't prepared to share equal treatment. Now he was glad of that company policy; for the first two years, the relationship between the two riders was quite cordial.

In his first year back, he managed to show he was not a spent force, including one win at Assen, round seven. Lorenzo was riding hurt, but all the same "it was one of my most special victories."

Overall, however, he was only the best of the rest in a year of Spanish domination. His home race at Misano was typical: Lorenzo, Marquez, and Pedrosa topped the rostrum, while Rossi was fourth, 15 seconds adrift. It was a disappointing end to a sentimental race at a track renamed after his late friend, Marco Simoncelli. Rossi's helmet adopted the words of a Pink Floyd song, "Wish You Were Here," carrying the lyrics: "How I wish, how I wish you were here./We're just two lost souls/Swimming in a fishbowl/Year after year/Running over the same old ground./What have we found?/The same old fears./Wish you were here."

The same three Spaniards dominated the title. Class rookie Marc Marquez was champion on his first attempt, at twenty-one the youngest ever; Lorenzo was just four points behind; Pedrosa placed, still close, in third. The trio had shared all the other race wins.

Rossi was fourth, almost 100 points adrift of Marquez. It seemed an honorable result. But Rossi saw himself differently. It wasn't nearly good enough. He needed a reset, and his radical solution took everyone by surprise.

↑

Rumor had Lorenzo being paid double what Rossi earned in 2013.

←

Teammate once more: Valentino rejoined Lorenzo at Yamaha in 2013. But now defending champion Jorge, here leaving the pits at Valencia, was the senior figure in the factory team.

IVECO
TT ASSEN
Assen 2013

↗
In 2013 Rossi returned to the top of the podium—this time at Assen—for the first time since leaving Yamaha for Ducati, ending what was by far the longest winless streak of his entire career. He is flanked by Marquez (left) and Cal Crutchlow.

→
After a humiliating two years with Ducati, Rossi was glad to be back with Yamaha.

He sacked his crew chief, Jeremy Burgess.

Together they had won seven World Championships, eighty races, and added another sixty-six podium finishes in fourteen years. The move smacked of desperation.

Nor did the way the news came out win many admirers. A leak within Rossi's "tribe" made headlines before Rossi had informed his longstanding ally. Burgess admitted, at a joint press conference called to smooth things over, that "I was blindsided."

Rossi had picked on the only major item he could change "to find new motivation," he said. "We have a great history—not just mechanical but also as part of the family. It was a very difficult decision."

Burgess took it on the chin, acknowledging that "We've spent the last four years chasing rainbows, and we haven't nailed many in that time." If it would return Rossi back to winning form, then it was the right decision. "I've read many sporting biographies where people coming to the end of their careers make changes like this—like a golfer changing his caddy." Asked privately in how many cases had the change worked, his reply was prompt. "None."

While the rest of the mainly antipodean crew stayed, Rossi already had the replacement crew chief lined up: fellow Italian Silvano Galbusera, a vastly experienced leader, having most recently run Yamaha's World Superbike team.

"Best of the rest" would take on a different meaning in 2014, as defending champion Marc Marquez embarked on a winning spree, taking the first ten races in a surge of Honda power and youthful exuberance, and adding three more in an eighteen-round season of utter dominance.

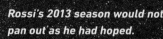

↗

Rossi's 2013 season would not pan out as he had hoped.

←

Rossi chats with F1 driver Lewis Hamilton.

↗

Rossi finished the 2013 season almost 100 points behind Honda's champion Marc Marquez.

→

Rossi, here with Kevin Schwantz, finished his first season back at Yamaha fourth overall, his worst apart from the Ducati years.

Had Rossi's crew shift worked? Seemingly yes, given the racing rule: the first person you must beat is your teammate. He and Lorenzo took two of the remaining wins apiece, but Rossi was stronger overall, with six second places and five thirds, only failing to score once when he crashed out at a rain-hit Aragon race.

All the better for his army of yellow-clad home-base fans, his first win was at Misano, and "better than Assen last year, where Lorenzo was injured." The next was at the beautiful Phillip Island in Australia. By this point, he'd regained second overall from Pedrosa.

Perhaps the change of crew chief was the anti-aging tonic he needed. Rossi's enthusiasm remained: when Yamaha tried to renew his contract for one more year in 2015, he declined. He insisted on two more.

The reason was curiosity, for in 2016 not only would new rules introduce control electronics for all riders, but Michelin was expected to replace Bridgestone as Yamaha's tire suppliers. "I think MotoGP will change very much . . . the crucial things, electronics and tires . . . with another kind of riding style and another way to control the bike. It is like Year Zero."

There was 2015 to finish up first. It was the year when relationships soured between the top riders, and Rossi missed a tenth title by a frustratingly slender five points.

It went not to the new boy wonder Marquez, who had a difficult season after Honda made some rare development missteps, but to his old Yamaha nemesis Jorge Lorenzo. And in a far from straightforward way. Fate had seemed to favor Valentino. In his third year back with Yamaha, it once again felt "like my bike." At Qatar's opening round he claimed a thrilling close win over Dovizioso and Iannone on the Ducatis. He won four of the first 15 of 18 races, and

↗

After a disappointing 2013 season, Rossi sacked his longtime crew chief, Jeremy Burgess.

←

For 2014 Rossi replaced Burgess with Italian Silvano Galbusera from Yamaha's World Superbike team, and the surprise switch seemed to work.

→

Marquez would win the first ten races of the 2014 season, all but mathematically eliminating his competition in the championship points race.

↓

A hug for the new superstar. Valentino congratulates new nemesis Marquez in 2014.

though Lorenzo had scored six, greater consistency put the veteran narrowly ahead on points, with three races to go.

It unraveled, as we saw earlier, in the Australian, Malaysian, and Valencian GPs. Valentino's last real chance of the championship was gone.

His Yamaha contract would expire at the end of 2016. At age 37, Valentino was the oldest on the grid and already a teenager when Marquez was born, and he was past the age when the competitive fires usually burn low. Wealthy beyond his dreams, with a record-breaking trophy cabinet, and still physically intact—surely this would be his last year?

He had other options. He'd passed up on Formula 1 chances with Ferrari, but enjoyed the rougher side of four-wheel motorsport, with top-15 places in World Championship rallies, promising results in endurance racing, and in 2016 took a record fifth win in the more light-hearted year-end Monza

Rally Show, against top competitors from several branches of motorsport. He could enjoy himself on four wheels, with less risk.

Once again, Valentino saw it differently. He signed up for another two years at Yamaha even before the first 2016 race. It was Lorenzo's turn to take offence and storm off to Ducati, declining to renew his Yamaha contract in favor of a megabucks deal for 2017.

The 2016 switch to Michelin tires added unpredictability as riders and engineers worked to adapt to a very different feel, with a record eight different winners in 18 races. Valentino was again a serious challenger, with two wins and eight further top-three results. Enough for second overall, beating Lorenzo. But the year belonged to Marquez for a third time, with five wins, and only one non-finish.

It might have been different, had Valentino's engine not blown up at Mugello, adding oil smoke to the clouds of yellow from the

← Rossi chats with former teammate Colin Edwards.

↓ New challengers kept the contest fresh, as Valentino started his third GP decade. Here future teammate Maverick Viñales, on the revitalised Suzuki, rides to a first premier-class victory at the 2016 British GP.

↑

Restart in the rain at Valencia in 2018. Valentino led then slipped off, remounting to finish 13th. Pursuers Dovizioso (Ducati, 4) and Rins (Suzuki) survived for first and second.

→

New colours for the last dance, Rossi rode in turquoise for the satellite Petronas team in 2021, but on a full factory bike.

fans. But he also crashed three times. In the end, he was 49 points adrift of Marquez. But still best of the rest.

And he was busy for 2017. His SKY VR46 team had expanded, adding two Moto2 entries to the Moto3 pair, and he was fending off questions about a potential move into MotoGP team ownership. And still racing well, after the first three races, in Qatar, Argentina, and the USA (a third and two seconds), he led the World Championship.

He had new opposition in his own garage. Rising 22-year-old Spaniard Maverick Viñales, fresh from a first win in 2016, had moved from Suzuki to replace Lorenzo, and won the first two races.

In round five at Le Mans, it came down to a last-lap battle. Rossi led but ran wide on the corner into the back straight. Viñales pounced. Rossi was ready for a counterattack in the last corners, but he never got there. Pushing a fraction too hard, he was down and out.

It was another year with unpredictable results. Valentino had to wait until the classic Dutch TT at Assen before taking

victory, his 115th, and as it transpired, his last. He would remain tantalizingly short of Giacomo Agostini's 122 wins.

By the half-year break, he was still in with a chance. Four riders, Marquez, Viñales, Dovizioso, and Rossi, were covered by just ten points.

It was still a struggle, however, adapting to the new tires. "I was never able to do two good races in a row," he said later. At round 12 at Silverstone a new chassis improved things, and he was back on the podium and just 17 points off ultimate winner Marquez.

Then—disaster. Trail riding near his Tavullia home, an awkward foot-down stop fractured both bones in his lower right leg. Supposed to be out for 30 days, he was back on his M1 after just 22, taking fifth at Aragon. He missed only one race. He was back on the podium two races later, second to Marquez in Australia—but it was too little too late, and he dropped to fifth overall.

The next season opened with another early signature, for 2019 and 2020, once again on the eve of the first round at Qatar. Two more years with the factory Yamaha

Lorenzo won the two races not won by Rossi or Marquez—here at Aragon.

Still talking . . . but later in 2015 an on-track altercation at Sepang broke the friendship, and a penalty ended Rossi's strongest title run in six years.

Even though Rossi and Lorenzo won two races apiece in 2014, Rossi finished ahead of Lorenzo in the points, proving he was not the second fiddle.

→
Something to celebrate. Rossi and Viñales share a podium party at the 2018 German GP. They had finished second and third, and they would be third and fourth in the championship.

team, and another pledge to reassess his position during 2020. Circumstances would cloud the issue.

The new season started promisingly—a close third in a three-way fight in the desert behind Dovizioso's Ducati and Marquez's Honda; and 2018 would again see a top-three title finish. It was, however, against the odds. The latest Yamaha had fallen behind the opposition—to the extent that Japanese project leader Kouji Tsuya issued an unprecedented apology to Rossi and Viñales after poor qualifying at Austria's ultra-fast Red Bull Ring. "We have to apologise to the riders because we have less ... acceleration performance right now," he said, clearly a painful moment. Rossi responded with

hopes the factory would now fix the issue: "It's a very long time I've spoken to them about the same problem—after one year we always have the same ..."

Even so, at that disadvantageous circuit, he fought through from 14th on the grid to sixth at the finish (Viñales was 11th). Still full of fire, on good days he could mix it with the best. Valentino came close to a single win in Malaysia, then crashed out under severe pressure from Marquez after 16 of 20 laps. Four more third places reflected sustained effort, but also an elevated level of competition. In his pomp, Rossi had been able to play with rivals to make a show, then win almost at will. Now he was at full stretch trying to keep up.

← After three podiums in his debut MotoGP season, double Moto2 champion Johann Zarco was another Yamaha rider inspired by Rossi ... and ready to challenge him too.

↓ Australia, 2017, and Valentino prepares for a practice gallop at Phillip Island, a favourite track, where he took seven of his 115 Grand Prix wins.

→ Innocent victim. Rossi runs off track and out of the race in a multiple crash at Montmelo in 2019, triggered by Lorenzo on the Repsol Honda. Viñales (centre, airborne) and Dovizioso (right) were also taken down.

↓ Circuit of the Americas in Texas, and Suzuki's Alex Rins hunts down leader Rossi. The order was reversed at the finish, with the Yamaha rider half-a-second down.

Machine weakness told even further in 2019. Rossi was still enjoying himself, and was twice second, in Argentina and the USA. Those were his only podiums, and while he could rely on the adulation of his fans, this was not the case with his motorcycle.

The latest M1 was extraordinarily sensitive to settings and to different conditions, and a real handful in hot weather and on slippery surfaces. His old ability for inspired setting changes on race mornings was not enough, and loyal fans had to share his disappointment at a string of bad results. Nor for once was luck on his side. A down-beat career-first struck when he crashed out of three consecutive races—at Mugello, Catalunya, and Assen. He was the innocent victim in the middle one, where Lorenzo also wiped out Dovizioso and Viñales. Those either side were unforced errors. Seventh overall

was his worst championship position since the Ducati doldrums.

But success for a great racing figure had already gained another dimension. His own racing teams, run under Rossi's close supervision by Pablo Nieto and his old friend Uccio, proved steadily improving status when Pecco Bagnaia, a friend and protégé, won the 2018 Moto2 World Championship after a close battle with rising Portuguese star Miguel Oliveira. At the same Malaysian GP where Pecco confirmed the win, Valentino's half-brother Luca Marini, riding the second SKY VR46 Kalex, claimed his first Grand Prix victory—some compensation for Valentino's crash out of the main event later that afternoon.

With one more year on his contract and hopes of adding another title undimmed, Valentino decided he needed a reset. It came in the form of another new crew chief.

←

Thicker than water ... Vale's half-brother Luca Marini sprays the bubbly after his first win, in Moto2 in Malaysia in 2018. The VR46 team's rider brought some consolation after Rossi crashed out of the lead in MotoGP.

→

The ever-growing championship trophy. Joan Mir, 2020 champion, relishes the addition of his name. The third row down belongs to Valentino.

↘

Inspired by Rossi, and ready to take over. Australian Jack Miller is a leading light of the new generation in MotoGP.

Out went Silvano Galbusera, seconded to the factory test team after the pair had taken nine wins in six seasons. In came the Spaniard who had engineered success in Moto2: David Muñoz. "He is young and has good ideas. With Pecco, I like the way he managed the end of the season, with a lot of pressure and Pecco was nervous. We will try, and see if we can become stronger," Valentino enthused.

Circumstances, however, were against him in 2020, an extraordinary season when the Covid pandemic delayed and truncated the calendar. Twenty scheduled races were cut back to just 14 for the premier class, all within Europe. In addition, Yamaha's latest iteration was as moody as before; and while satellite-team rider Fabio Quartararo managed three wins on it in only his second year, and Rossi's factory teammate Viñales

one, Valentino struggled. (Valentino's close friend and protégé Franco Morbidelli also managed three Yamaha wins, riding a year-old model.)

In line for at least a top-five in the title, it all went wrong when he crashed out of the second of two races at his home Misano circuit. A week later in Catalunya he was a strong second when he crashed out again. Then at Le Mans he fell victim to the notorious turn two on the first lap—a third consecutive non-finish. And then it got worse. Diagnosed with Covid, he missed the next two races altogether. It added up to his worst championship position in any class: 15th.

He wasn't done yet. Still feeling competitive, and retaining at least some of Yamaha's faith, his contract had been renewed for another year, but not with the factory

↑
Pupil leads teacher. Satellite-team Yamaha rider Franco Morbidelli leads factory rider Rossi at the San Marino GP, en route to his first premier-class win. Rossi was a close mentor and closer friend to the younger rider.

Make an appointment with The Doctor

BRITISH MOTO GP

29 August 2021

↑
Fans' favorite Rossi was in his last season, but still the iconic image of MotoGP. He was chosen to promote the British GP at Silverstone in 2021.

team. Instead, he would swap with new bright hope Quartararo, trading the blue Monster Yamaha livery for the turquoise of the Petronas SRT satellite team. He would however have a full factory bike. "Not much will change except the color," Valentino cheerfully proclaimed. But there was more: although crew chief Muñoz and faithful electronics engineer Matteo Flamigni went with him, there was no room for others in his long-serving pit crew, and stalwart figures Bernard Ansiau, Alex Briggs, and Brent Stevens were out, the latter two leaving MotoGP for racing in Australia.

Valentino's last year was a farewell tour to remember. Not for the results, but for the response of the fans. The love was tangible. Over 18 rounds in a slightly less constricted but still Covid-hit season (they raced in Qatar and in the USA this time) Quartararo took the championship for Yamaha, while Valentino finished a worst-ever 18th overall, with just four top-ten finishes all season. But after the final race in Valencia, it was not Fabio who was cheered to the echo by an adoring capacity crowd, and for whom all the other riders stopped on the slow-down lap for a final moment of congratulation.

The year had started with the repeated assurance, that "if I feel competitive and am enjoying racing, I will decide whether to stay." The pleasure of riding a 250-horsepower bike to the limit remained undimmed, but the enjoyment was undermined by the results.

Valentino wasn't going any slower. A comparison of qualifying times at four directly comparable circuits shows that he was in fact quicker in Portugal and Austria, slower at Jerez and Misano—in each case by small margins. But the others, the newer riders, were all going faster.

The ageing former master of different disciplines—from 125 through 250 to 500, to MotoGP, from two-stroke to four-stroke, from Aprilia to Honda to Yamaha—was finally finding it harder to adapt to developing technology. The youngsters, with

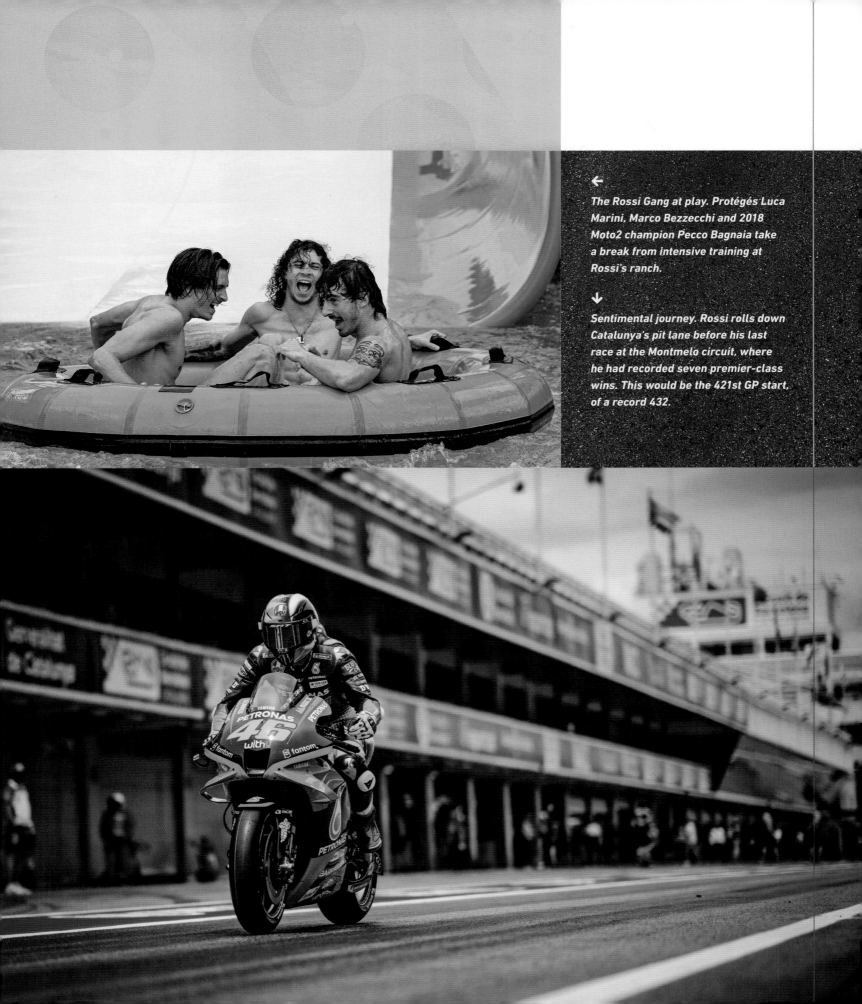

The Rossi Gang at play. Protégés Luca Marini, Marco Bezzecchi and 2018 Moto2 champion Pecco Bagnaia take a break from intensive training at Rossi's ranch.

↓

Sentimental journey. Rossi rolls down Catalunya's pit lane before his last race at the Montmelo circuit, where he had recorded seven premier-class wins. This would be the 421st GP start, of a record 432.

→

Behind every good man, a good woman. Valentino's fiance, Italian model Francesca Sofia Novello, break cover in Qatar in 2021

no prior history or preconceptions, were coming up with different techniques. Valentino had too much existing knowledge to be able to join in.

There were other factors.

In 26 Grand Prix years his worst injury had been a broken leg. He missed four races but came back strong as ever. But in 2020 in Austria, he had a miraculous escape from a terrifying incident that might easily have taken his life. Tailing teammate Viñales through Turn 3 when, a hundred odd yards behind, Johann Zarco and Franco Morbidelli collided at close to top speed. Their two bikes came somer-

saulting through the air, over the heads of Rossi and Viñales. They missed by a matter of feet. It was more than very sobering.

His personal life had also moved on, with a deepening commitment to his girlfriend since late 2018, Milanese model Francesca Sofia Novello—and in August the couple confirmed that she was expecting their daughter. Real life, Part Two.

The factors all added up. It was time to call it a day. And at a packed special conference at the Red Bull Ring on August 5, 2021, Valentino announced that he was going to retire at the end of the year.

Inches from disaster. Morbidelli's Yamaha cartwheels to destruction, passing between the bikes of Viñales and Rossi in Austria in 2021. A split second later, Zarco's bike looped overhead. It was a sobering moment.

Rossi's feet couldn't touch the ground after his final race in Valencia—his team, fan club and a host of pit lane supporters made sure of that.

CHAPTER 13

TAVULLIA: ROSSI PAINTS THE TOWN YELLOW

It's often the case that exceptionally successful sportsmen can't wait to shake off the dust of their humble hometown origins, if only for tax reasons. Monaco is full of such people, and the nightclubs of London, Paris, and New York have their share as well.

Tricolore house and the words of a champion. Many more would follow.

Baby Fiats are even cuter when they've been given the Valentino touch.

In other Italian country towns, you might find laundry hanging out. In Tavullia, it's bunting for its favorite son.

Rossi has shown he is not averse to such nightclubs. He keeps his private life very private, but he's also a noted party animal. For a time, he also enjoyed his tax-friendly part-time residence in London, until that arrangement went south.

Still, he was brought up in Tavullia, and that town remains the center of his universe. It's also the center of his empire, with the headquarters of his VR46 Apparel organization and his VR46 Training Ranch just a few miles outside of town, with senior staff drawn from the friends of his youth.

The coast of the Rimini Riviera is mainly devoted to budget holidays: inexpensive hotels and apartments line the beaches, lapped by the generally calm waters of the Adriatic. In holiday season, the place heaves with people, spilling out of the bars and clubs, pizzerias, and gelaterias.

Travel only a couple of miles inland into the hilly countryside and you could almost be in a different country. Traditional hilltop towns with crazily narrow streets are set among gentle pastoral fields. Tavullia is one such hill town.

It is here that Rossi first formed the bonds that have survived and strengthened ever since. This is home to his "tribe."

To call him a local hero would be far short of the truth. Visit the town and—even without noting the number of buildings painted yellow and his fan club's headquarters next to the church—you'll see his flags, his presence, and his number 46 everywhere.

There is even a Pizzeria da Rossi, along with a gelateria attached to the fan club. Nowadays, though, with the town a Mecca to his vast army of fans, it's not so easy

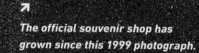

↗
The official souvenir shop has grown since this 1999 photograph.

←
If everything is yellow, then you know you are in Tavullia. Rossi owns the color, and the town.

for Rossi to enjoy strolling along the steep cobbled streets without being accosted for a selfie or an autograph.

Rossi's commercial empire has as its core a group of old friends, the people who accompanied him to his earliest races before he became famous. They also form the core of the gang that marches from Tavullia to the Misano circuit for the San Marino Grand Prix every year. There they swell the number of yellow-clad fans splashing the trademark color across entire grandstands.

The VR46 Apparel company, with its thirty-strong staff, is housed in a modern building a couple of kilometers outside of Tavullia; the structure is highlighted by a circular main section clad in mirrored glass. While old friends like CEO Albi Tebaldi and the younger Gianluca Falcioni manage details, Rossi still takes a personal interest, applying his own strong sense of style most particularly to his own merchandising items.

As well as his holiday home in Ibiza, Rossi's purpose-built villa on the outskirts of Tavullia is his own private headquarters. His life in London is a distant memory: home for Valentino is where the heart is. And that is in Tavullia.

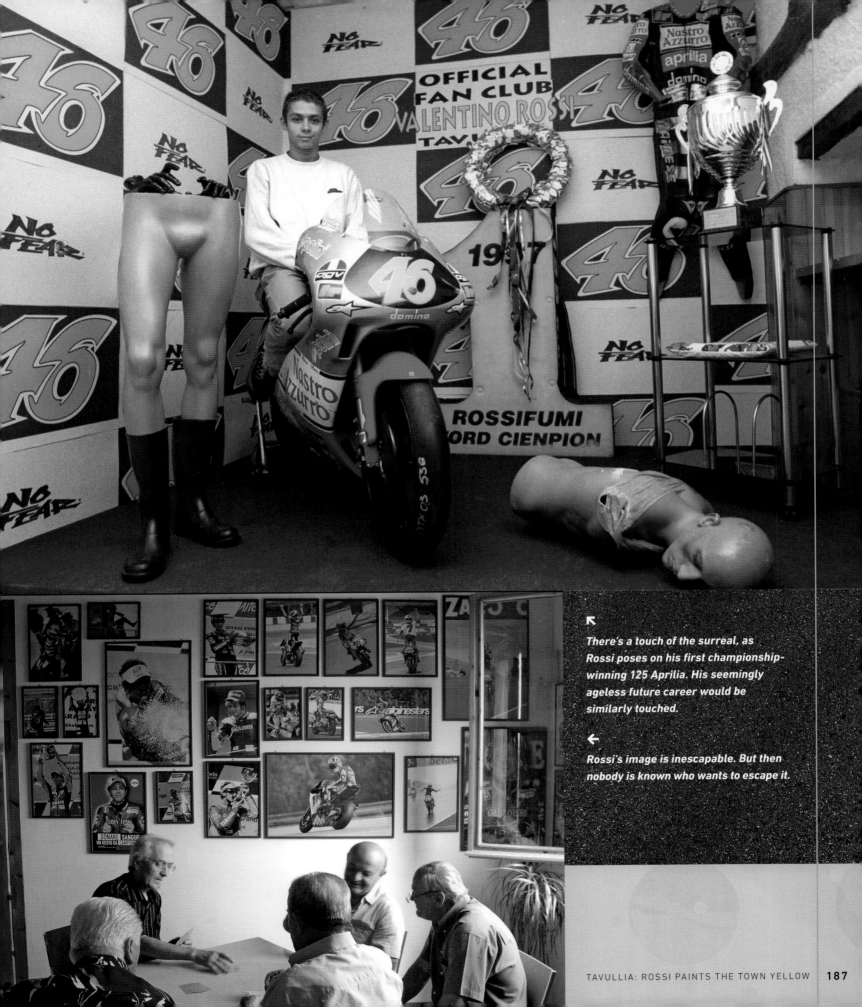

There's a touch of the surreal, as Rossi poses on his first championship-winning 125 Aprilia. His seemingly ageless future career would be similarly touched.

Rossi's image is inescapable. But then nobody is known who wants to escape it.

CHAPTER 14

PASSING ON THE BATON

The ground-floor conference room at Austria's lavish Red Bull Ring was packed and buzzing, for what was billed as "an exceptional press conference." It fell silent as Valentino walked in, with a slightly quizzical smile.

→

An ageless thirty-eight, Valentino made the front row of the grid at the Circuit of the Americas, along with youngsters Maverick Viñales (left) and triple champion Marc Marquez in 2017.

↗
Pupil leads master: rising Italian star Franco Morbidelli is just one of the riders taking benefit from Rossi's patronage and tuition at the Ranch.

→
"Go for win number ten!" A Spanish fan of the Doctor at Jerez celebrates that he's won there nine times already.

Circuit of the Americas 2017

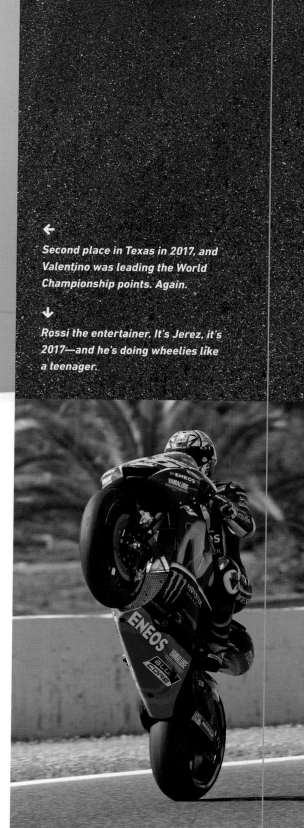

← Second place in Texas in 2017, and Valentino was leading the World Championship points. Again.

↓ Rossi the entertainer. It's Jerez, it's 2017—and he's doing wheelies like a teenager.

Everyone was pretty sure what he was going to say. They'd been waiting 26 years for it. But the impact was in no way lessened, as the greatest rider of his time broke the news.

"Hi everybody," he began. "Like I said during the season, I would take my decision after the summer break. And I decide to stop. Unfortunately, this will be my last season as a MotoGP rider ..."

At the start of the year, he had still hoped he might continue into 2022, another attempt to add a tenth title, a 116th race win, a 200th premier-class podium. "But I needed to understand if I was fast enough. During the season our results were less than what I expect. Race by race I started to think.

"It is difficult, and a very sad moment. Next year my life will change. But anyway—it was great. I enjoy very much, but in all the sports, the results make the difference, so in the end it is the right way. I am a little bit sad not to get the tenth championship. I think I deserve this, with my level and my speed. I lose two times in the last race. But anyway, I think I can be happy with my results in my career."

Most of all, he said, he would miss riding a MotoGP bike, with a revealing insight into the depth of the experience. "It is always a great emotion. I will miss a lot Sunday morning, two hours before the race. It's something where you don't feel comfortable. You are scared, but it's

→ *Rossi at play. But even the games are dedicated to improving his skill: dirt-tracking is perfect practice for good throttle control.*

↓ *The nose of the beast: Rossi's decal-decorated 2017 Yamaha M1.*

an emotion because you know the race starts."

Of all his achievements, to Rossi one other aspect stood out: "A lot of people followed motorcycles because of me," he said. "This is the most important thing I did in my career."

The moment triggered an outpouring of accolades and devotion, both in the paddock and far, far beyond. Both friends and rivals joined the tributes, for what old foe Max Biaggi (among others) called "the end of an era." Rossi, to the benefit of all, had transcended the sport, and everybody knew it.

And he wasn't going away.

For his own part, he planned to continue racing on four wheels. He'd turned his back on Formula 1 chances, despite impressive tests with Ferrari in 2006, 2008 and 2010, and a run in Lewis Hamilton's Mercedes in 2019. But past success in World Championship rallies in New Zealand and Wales confirmed a strong aptitude; while he is seven times winner of the Monza Rally Show, an annual fun event for top-level competitors from many branches of motor sport. He had set a competitive lap time in a NASCAR run in 2013 and achieved worthwhile finishes in occasional outings in the Blancpain GT World Challenge Europe series. This would be his first destination. In January of 2022 he signed up to a full ten-race season in the series, comprising both sprint and endurance races, driving a Team WRT Audi R8.

There could be little doubt however that Valentino would remain a major presence in bike racing, where his several senior roles

Yellow smoke bombs, yellow on the tire wall, and Rossi on his back wheel. He pleases the crowd at the French GP in 2017.

Pleasantries and pressure. As team boss, Valentino welcomed his Moto2 rider Pecco Bagnaia to the pre-event conference at Misano in September. Bagnaia went on to win the race, and two months later the championship.

↑

The next generation in 2018. Graduates from Rossi's training ranch now competing in his teams. Moto2 riders Bagnaia (left) and Marini flank the Moto3 gang, from left Dennis Foggia, Celestino Vietti and Nicolo Bulega.

→

The hero at home in Italy. Mugello is a favorite track for him and his fans.

had already achieved maturity. There were two major elements: as a team owner, and as a talent-spotting training ringmaster.

The VR46 team was launched in 2014, with Uccio Salucci and Pablo Nieto (son of legendary 50/125cc multi-champion Angel Nieto) sharing management duties. At first, the enterprise, sponsored by Italian TV corporation SKY, was just in Moto3. By 2017, Rossi had added a SKY VR46 Moto2 team, and the professional approach demonstrated serious intent. And in 2018 Francesco "Pecco" Bagnaia won eight races and secured the Moto2 World Championship.

In 2021 came the move to MotoGP. The Moto3 team was temporarily withdrawn, and the Tavullia squad had taken advantage of the fact that an established MotoGP team, the Spanish Esponsorama squad, had run into sponsorship problems.

Esponsorama retained one of their two grid slots and ceded the second one to VR46.

Bagnaia had by now joined the factory Ducati team; Vale's half-brother Luca Marini moved up from Moto2 to MotoGP, along with key members of the VR46 racing empire, sharing Ducati machinery and a pit box with Esponsorama. It was auspicious enough. Marini scored points in 11 of 18 rounds, including two top-tens, with a best of fifth in the rain in Austria. He finished 19th overall, three points and one position behind his older sibling.

For 2022, another step forward. Esponsorama left the class, VR46 achieved fully independent status, taking two grid slots. With Pablo Nieto now managing both entries, Marini would be joined by 2020 Moto2 title runner-up Marco Bezzecchi,

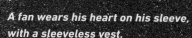

↗
A fan wears his heart on his sleeve, with a sleeveless vest.

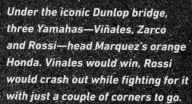

←

Under the iconic Dunlop bridge, three Yamahas—Viñales, Zarco and Rossi—head Marquez's orange Honda. Vinales would win, Rossi would crash out while fighting for it with just a couple of corners to go.

both riding Ducatis. After an on-again/off-again saga with Saudi sponsorship from Aramco, it was finally confirmed that Italian banking concern Mooney would be backing the Rossi teams in both MotoGP and Moto2, where they were to field two more Valentino protégés: Celestino Vietti and Nico Antonelli.

All these riders, plus several others including strong MotoGP title challenger Bagnaia, had something else in common—they were graduates of Valentino's own VR46 Academy, which over the past decade or so had matured to become a racers' training ground of unprecedented power and influence.

Core of the VR46 Riders Academy is The Ranch, where a state-of-the-art dirt-track, comprising several layouts, is in daily use, as a vital component of any rid-

er's training program. "First of all," explains Valentino, "it is difficult to organize training on asphalt." Permanent circuits like Misano and Mugello were available, but not every day, "or even every week." Secondly, "on the dirt, you have a lot less grip. You have to move on the seat to improve the grip, control the throttle … these are important things to improve your skill on the asphalt."

The dirt-track name harks back to its inspiration—Kenny Roberts Sr.'s training ranches, one at his home in California and another built for Dorna in Barcelona in the 1990s.

The essential ingredient is a loose dirt-track surface, smooth and carefully maintained. Here riders can learn how to skate the front wheel, spin the rear, and slide around corners, using their weight

↑

Rossi had a bad day in Catalunya, dropping to eighth—but his congratulations to winning compatriot Andrea Dovizioso (Ducati) were warm and sincere. Better him than one of those Honda riders!

→

Final season—yet to decide his future, Rossi practises for the Qatar GP in 2021, first time out in satellite-team colours. Disappointing results finally made up his mind.

An elder statesman on matters of track safety, Rossi examines a revised corner at Montmelo in Catalunya in 2017.

Pushing off for combat at Mugello in 2017. Qualified second, Vale finished fourth.

↗

Tucked and going for gold: Rossi at the Dutch TT in 2017—where he took his 115th and final Grand Prix win.

→

It doesn't get any easier. Rossi is pressed hard by fellow-Italian Danilo Petrucci's Ducati on the way to his win. Lapped rider Hector Barbera gives them plenty of space.

and precise throttle control to make fine adjustments to the bike's attitude and balance. All while trying to go faster than the next man.

Even at the slower speeds of a tight track, it requires courage, commitment, and finesse in extreme conditions. Exactly the elements required for Grand Prix racing, especially when a rider graduates to the powerful MotoGP category, where the same things happen at much higher speed and intensity. Motocross can teach balance and endurance, gym work and cycling can polish fitness, diet and discipline can maximize physical responses, and obsessive determination can create the will to win. But there is nothing like dirt-tracking, hour after hour for day after day, to learn how to be good at Grand Prix road-racing.

Though nobody has had as much fun at the Ranch as Valentino, it was not a purely self-indulgent exercise, but a response to an unexpected dearth of young Italian talent after the turn of the century.

The nation had once vied for domination with Great Britain, as a mainstay of Grand Prix motorcycle racing from its inception in 1949. After Rossi, though, the supply of talent seemed to dry up. In its place, a new generation of Spanish riders. The first Spanish premier-class champion had been Alex Criville in 1999. In his wake, in increasing numbers came the likes of Alvaro Bautista, Dani Pedrosa, Jorge Lorenzo, and a substantial supporting cast. It was no accident. Formal talent-spotting programs and well-sponsored junior race series had created a conveyer belt. In 2010 all three titles went to Spanish riders: Marc Marquez in 125, Toni Elias in Moto2, and Lorenzo in MotoGP. The feat was repeated in 2013 (Viñales, Pol Espargaro, Marquez).

Rain at Assen means treaded tires, a rear safety light, and another chance for the old warhorse to shine.

Valentino consults with long-time crewman Bernard Ansiau in Italy. By 2017, they'd been working together for fourteen years.

Rossi had seen the writing on the wall. He knew it wasn't talent that was missing in Italy, but a lack of opportunity and focused training, for a sporting discipline that was becoming more specialized year by year. "The target is to find young Italian riders and develop their talent, to give them the chance to shine," he explained.

Thus, the VR46 Academy was formed, loosely at first, in 2014. Gradually it became more formal as its role extended, with several graduates moving into the World Championships. Among them, World Champions Bagnaia and Franco Morbidelli, serial Grand Prix winners including Nico Antonelli, Lorenzo Baldassarri, Marco Bezzecchi, Luca Marini, and Andrea Migno, along with other notables including Stefano Manzi and Nicolo Bulega.

The essential purpose evolved. Rossi had already provided the inspiration, and now also the means to elevate a new gen-eration of Italian riders, to take on where he would inevitably one day leave off. This project was already well advanced by the time he retired. It had expanded to host training camps for chosen Yamaha riders, as well as forming new links across the breadth of racing.

Dirt-track training was first popularized by triple 500cc World Champion Roberts in the late 1970s. He was the pioneer of a platoon of American talent who would take a dominant role through the 1980s and into the 1990s. Along with a handful of Australians, they had all polished their skills riding dirt-track. As power outputs rose to overcome the grip of the rear tires, they were able to take advantage. European riders were forced to take note.

Rossi himself learned how to ride fast on impromptu dirt-tracks in a local quarry. This was thanks in large part to his father

↑
A familiar sight as Rossi lifts the winner's trophy. But it had been more than year since the last when he won in the Netherlands in 2017.

→
The Assen grandstand echoes to cheering every time The Doctor goes by.

↗
The taste of winning never gets less enjoyable. Rossi at the Dutch TT in 2017.

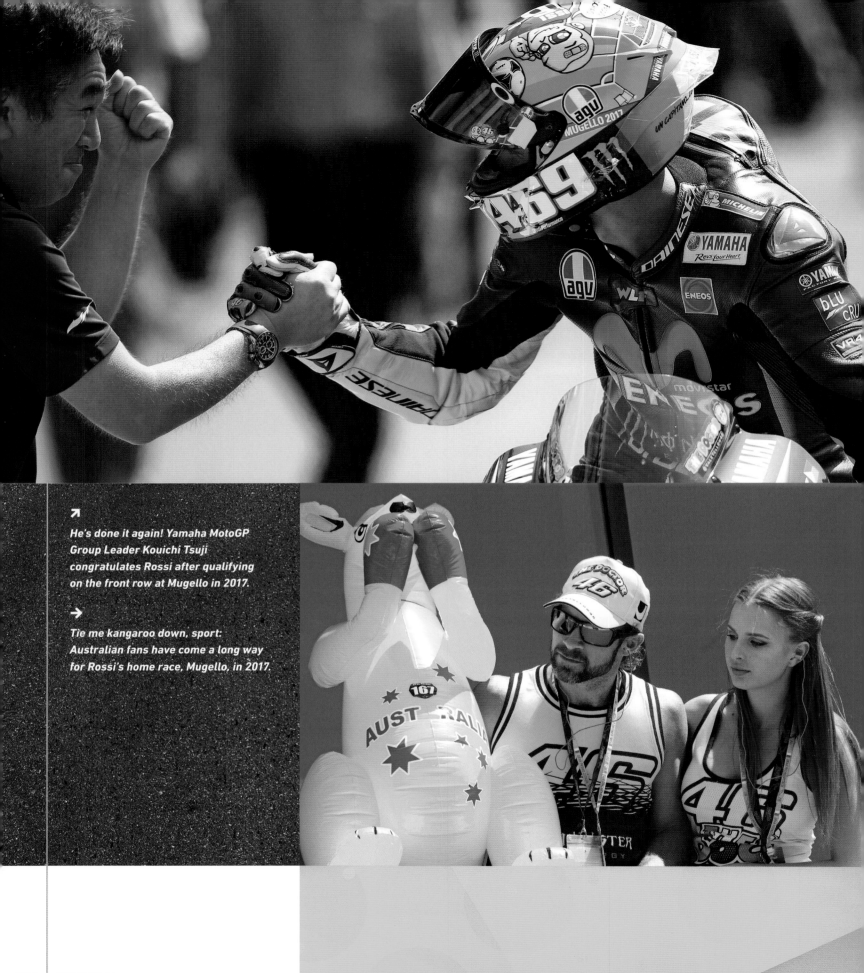

↗
He's done it again! Yamaha MotoGP
Group Leader Kouichi Tsuji
congratulates Rossi after qualifying
on the front row at Mugello in 2017.

→

Tie me kangaroo down, sport:
Australian fans have come a long way
for Rossi's home race, Mugello, in 2017.

Graziano's farsighted understanding of modern racing, as well as the simple desire to have fun on wheels with his son. The Ranch formalized similar opportunities for the next generation.

The land, almost 200 acres, was bought by Graziano with just such a plan in mind, and it started to take shape around 2012. The property includes vineyards and olive trees, but these are only incidental. More important is a bunkhouse, providing comfort and accommodation and a raucous dining hall, and a forum to dissect the experiences of the day. As the youngsters must learn, racing is not just the ability to ride fast. It is also vital to understand why you are going fast, to listen to other opinions about technique, and to be able to find new ways to go even faster.

The dirt-track basically comprises two concentric ovals, surrounded by a sinuous 1.8-km "TT circuit," with corners of differing radius and in different directions. A number of layouts are possible, ranging from conventional left-turn-only ovals to tracks with elevation changes, tighter and looser corners, ess-bends, sweepers and hairpins.

It is a playground in daily use by Rossi, along with, at various times, many MotoGP riders, even from outside his immediate circle. Rossi's tribe is in frequent attendance, and informal events include the annual "Ranch 100-Km Race" for friends and fellow travelers.

Davide Brivio, a longtime associate who had originally lured Rossi from Honda to Yamaha in 2003 and who worked for many

↑

Win number 115, at Assen in 2017, put Rossi just seven wins short of Agostini's all-time record.

←

Tribute to a legend. After his final race at Valencia, Rossi stopped trackside to say goodbye to the fans, and all his fellow riders spontaneously drew up alongside him.

↑

Bike racing finally over, Rossi embraces "Real Life—Part Two", with his pregnant girlfriend Francesca Sofia Novello. In mid-August of 2021, they announced they were expecting a daughter.

↗

A picture worth a thousand words. At Rossi's last MotoGP race in Valencia, the wall of the control tower wore a mural of his face. The effect was breathtaking.

years in the VR46 empire, was involved from the start. At the beginning, according to Brivio, "the selection was quite . . . based on request. He was not seeking out special riders, but more or less friends. The first were riders living around there."

Valentino had created his own system, Brivio explained: his personal trainer, his testing track, a lawyer for contracts. He had a merchandising company. He had a network around him for his own activity. The romantic idea is that the system is available to the young talent who want to become professional MotoGP riders. So, riders even 14 or 15 years old, riding in the Italian championship, can use Valentino's coaching, his trainer, his testing track, consultation with the lawyer, and merchandising . . . etc.

But rather than a money-making venture for the VR46 empire, it was more an investment for the future, Brivio said. "This is one activity where Valentino is actually spending money. My feeling is that the Academy is doing what a sport federation should do. Or what Dorna has done."

It also serves another purpose, he added, before Rossi's retirement. "In the

end—this is my personal opinion—the academy is helping to keep Valentino younger. He is living every day, going to the gym with these young kids; he goes to the ranch challenging them. This keeps him younger. Of course, they want to beat Valentino Rossi, and he has to defend."

Motorcycles for Rossi are about having fun; and having fun is about maximizing your performance to get better, get faster ... and have more fun. That's why every training session inevitably ends up in a race. Who better to pass on his decades of race-craft?

It's hard to think of a Grand Prix racing paddock without Valentino Rossi. From his first arrival—a mop-headed teenager whose speed and ebullient personality made him impossible to overlook—to his final race at Valencia in November, 2021, he has personified his sport, and won admirers everywhere. Naturally gifted, commercially astute, devastatingly dedicated, intrinsically charming, powerfully popular ... and loving every minute of it.

Now, on the brink of fatherhood, he had retired to become an elder statesman.

The Valentino Phenomenon.

APPENDIX

	VALENTINO ROSSI GRAND PRIX RESULTS							
YEAR	CLASS	MACHINE	STARTS	WINS	TOP THREE	POLE	FL	CHAMP POSITION
1996	125cc	Aprilia RS125	15	1	2	1	2	9
1997	125cc	Aprilia RS125	15	11	13	4	7	1
	125 Class Totals		**30**	**12**	**15**	**5**	**9**	
1998	250cc	Aprilia RS250	14	5	9	0	3	2
1999	250cc	Aprilia RS250	16	9	12	5	8	1
	250 Class Totals		**30**	**14**	**21**	**5**	**11**	
2000	500cc	Honda NSR500	16	2	10	0	5	2
2001	500cc	Honda NSR500	16	11	13	4	10	1
2002	MotoGP	Honda RC211V	16	11	15	7	9	1
2003	MotoGP	Honda RC211V	16	9	16	9	12	1
2004	MotoGP	Yamaha M1	16	9	11	5	3	1
2005	MotoGP	Yamaha M1	17	11	16	5	6	1
2006	MotoGP	Yamaha M1	17	5	10	5	4	2
2007	MotoGP	Yamaha M1	18	4	8	4	3	3
2008	MotoGP	Yamaha M1	18	9	16	2	5	1
2009	MotoGP	Yamaha M1	17	6	13	7	6	1
2010	MotoGP	Yamaha M1	14	2	10	1	2	3
2011	MotoGP	Ducati GP11	17	0	1	0	1	7
2012	MotoGP	Ducati GP12	18	0	2	0	1	6
2013	MotoGP	Yamaha M1	18	1	6	0	1	4
2014	MotoGP	Yamaha M1	18	2	13	1	1	2
2015	MotoGP	Yamaha M1	18	4	15	1	4	2
2016	MotoGP	Yamaha M1	18	2	10	3	2	2
2017	MotoGP	Yamaha M1	17	1	6	0	0	5
2018	MotoGP	Yamaha M1	18	0	5	1	0	3
2019	MotoGP	Yamaha M1	19	0	2	0	1	7
2020	MotoGP	Yamaha M1	12	0	1	0	0	15
2021	MotoGP	Yamaha M1	18	0	0	0	0	18
	500/MotoGP Class Totals		**372**	**89**	**199**	**55**	**76**	
	GRAND TOTALS		**432**	**115**	**235**	**65**	**96**	

OTHER PREMIER-CLASS STATISTICS

Total 500/MotoGP points scored

1	Valentino Rossi	5,415
2	Dani Pedrosa	2,976
3	Jorge Lorenzo	2,899
4	Andrea Dovizioso	2,568
5	Marc Marquez	2,417

Greatest number of 500/MotoGP Starts

1	Valentino Rossi	372
2	Alex Barros	246
3	Andrea Dovizioso	234
4 =	Nicky Hayden	218
	Dani Pedrosa	

Most consecutive 500/MotoGP Starts

1	Andrea Dovizioso	229
2	Valentino Rossi	170
3	Alex Barros	158
4 =	Colin Edwards	141
	Alvaro Bautista	

Most consecutive 500/MotoGP Podiums

1	Valentino Rossi	23
2	Giacomo Agostini	22
3	Casey Stoner	19
4	Mick Doohan	17
5 =	Valentino Rossi	16
	Marc Marquez	

Results from FIM MotoGP Results / Dorna / Wikiwand / motorsportstats.com

Notes
MotoGP: 990cc from 2002 to 2006, 800cc from 2007 to 2011, 1000cc from 2012 to 2021
FL: Fastest Lap

INDEX

PHOTO CREDITS

ABOUT THE AUTHOR

South Africa-born Michael Scott has been a journalist for fifty years, specializing in motorcycles for forty of them, and has covered motorcycle Grand Prix racing full-time since 1984. He has reported on Rossi's career from his debut to the present day, and has watched him grow from boy to man through a regular series of one-on-one interviews and feature stories. Combining technical understanding with a fascination for the depth of the personalities involved, Scott is author of several books about motorcycle racing. Titles include important histories of the World Championships, as well as best-selling biographies of former World Champions Wayne Rainey and Barry Sheene. He has been editor of the prestigious and authoritative annual "Bible of Motorcycle Racing," *Motocourse*, since 1991.